Connections Student Notebook

for

Rathus's

Psychology

Concepts and Connections

Ninth Edition

Connections Student Notebook

for

Rathus's

Psychology

Concepts and Connections

Ninth Edition

THOMSON
WADSWORTH

Australia • Canada • Mexico • Singapore • Spain • United Kingdom • United States

Printed in the United States of America
1 2 3 4 5 6 7   08 07 06 05 04

Printer: Thomson/West

ISBN: 0-534-46304-5

For more information about our products, contact us at:
Thomson Learning Academic Resource Center
1-800-423-0563

For permission to use material from this text or product, submit a request online at
http://www.thomsonrights.com

Any additional questions about permissions can be submitted by email to
thomsonrights@thomson.com

Thomson Wadsworth
10 Davis Drive
Belmont, CA 94002-3098
USA

Asia
Thomson Learning
5 Shenton Way #01-01
UIC Building
Singapore 068808

Australia/New Zealand
Thomson Learning
102 Dodds Street
Southbank, Victoria 3006
Australia

Canada
Nelson
1120 Birchmount Road
Toronto, Ontario M1K 5G4
Canada

Europe/Middle East/South Africa
Thomson Learning
High Holborn House
50/51 Bedford Row
London WC1R 4LR
United Kingdom

Latin America
Thomson Learning
Seneca, 53
Colonia Polanco
11560 Mexico D.F.
Mexico

Spain/Portugal
Paraninfo
Calle/Magallanes, 25
28015 Madrid, Spain

Table of Contents

Preface

Dear Student:

The Connections Student Notebook is designed to help you take study notes as you read Rathus's *Psychology: Concepts and Connections, 9th edition* and as you attend your psychology lectures. In this notebook, you will find "PowerVisuals" or some select figures from your text. The PowerVisuals are structured so that you can quiz yourself while taking notes. Interactive versions of these visuals are also available on the Book Companion Web Site for the Rathus text. Good luck in your psychology course.

The publisher would like to thank Krista Forrest of the University Nebraska. The outlines in this notebook are from a Microsoft® PowerPoint® presentation written by Dr. Forrest for this text.

Chapter 1: What is Psychology?

Defining Psychology

- Psychology is defined as the scientific study of behavior and mental processes.

Psychology as a Science

- Theories:
  - formulations of apparent relationships among observed events.

What Psychologists do

- Pure research
- Applied research
- Practice psychology
- Teaching

Fields of Psychology

- Clinical psychologists
- Counseling psychologists
- School psychologists
- Educational psychologists
- Developmental psychologists
- Personality psychologists
- Social psychologists
- Environmental psychologists
- Experimental psychologists
- Industrial psychologists
- Organizational psychologists
- Human factors psychologists
- Consumer psychologists
- Health psychologists
- Sport psychologists

Where Psychology Comes From: A History

Philosophical Contributions

- Aristotle: (384-322 BCE)
- Democritus (around 400 BCE)
- Plato (ca.427-347 BCE)

19th Century Contributions

- Gustav Theodore Fechner (1801-1887)
- Wilhelm Wundt (1832-1920)

Structuralism and Functionalism

- Structuralism
  - Attempts to break conscious experience down into
    - objective sensations such as sight, or taste, and
    - the subjective feelings such as emotional responses.
  - Believes that the mind functions by combining objective and subjective elements of experience.

- Functionalism
  - In the study of individuals the focus should be on behavior as well as the mind and consciousness.

Behaviorism: Practicing Psychology in Public
John Broadus Watson (1878-1958)
  - Believed that psychology should limit itself to observable, measurable events and behavior.

- B.F. Skinner (1904-1990)
  - Believed organisms learn to behave in certain ways because of reinforcement.

Gestalt Psychology: Making Psychology Whole

- Gestalt translates to "pattern" or "organized whole".

- Demonstrated that learning is a accomplished by insight, not by mechanical repetition.

- Founders included:
  - Wertheimer (1880-1943),
  - Koffka (1886-1941), and
  - Kohler (1887-1967).

Psychoanalysis: Digging beneath the surface

- Focus on the unconscious - a seething cauldron of conflicting impulses, urges and wishes.
  - Founded by Sigmund Freud.
  - Often called psychodynamic.

How Today's Psychologists
View Behavior and Mental Processes.

The Evolutionary and Biological Perspectives

- Focus on the evolution of behavior and mental processes.

- Genes can be transmitted from generation to generation.

- Biological perspective seek the links between the electrical and chemical activity of the brain.

The Cognitive Perspective

- Venture into the realm of mental processes to understand human nature.

- Cognitive psychologists study those things we refer to as the mind.

The Humanistic-Existential Perspective.

- Humanism
  - stresses the human capacity for self-fulfillment.

- Existentialism
  - views people as free to choose and be responsible for choosing ethical conduct.

- Humanistic-Existential psychologists stress the importance of subjective experience.
  - Abraham Maslow and Carl Rogers; two prominent psychologists in this area.

The Psychodynamic Perspective

- Freud's influence continues to be felt though contemporary psychodynamic theorists would likely call themselves neoanalysts.

- Famous neoanalysts include:
  - Karen Horney (1885-1952), and
  - Erik Erikson (1902-1994),
  - Former APA president Dorothy Cantor.

Perspectives on Learning

- Learning through repetition and reinforcement.

- Social-cognitive theorists
  - (formerly termed social learning theorists)
  - suggest that people can modify or even create their environments.
  - Intentional learning by observing others.

The Sociocultural Perspective

- Addresses the many ways in which people differ from one another.

- Study influences of ethnicity, gender, culture, and socioeconomic status on behavior and mental processes.
  - Ethnicity
    - Ethnic groups are united by their cultural heritage, race, language, and common history.
    - Study cultural heritages and ethnic differences in vulnerability to problems.
  - Gender
    - Refers to the culturally defined concepts of masculinity and femininity.
    - Involves a complex web of cultural expectations and social roles.

Gender, Ethnicity, and Psychology: Real People in the Real World

- Mary Whiton Calkins (1863-1930).

- Christine Ladd-Franklin (1847-1930).

- Margaret Floy Washburn (1871-1939).

- Helen Bradford Thompson (1874-1947).

- Today more than half of American college students are women.

- Nearly 3/4 of the undergraduate degrees in psychology and 2/3 of the doctoral degrees are earned by women.

- 1901 Gilbert Haven Jones, an African American, received his Ph.D. in psychology in Germany.

- Kenneth Clark and Mamie Philips Clark.

- Jorge Sanchez was among the first to show how intelligence tests are culturally biased.

- 6% of first year doctoral students are African American, 6% are Asian American, 5% are Latino and about 1% are Native American.

The Scientific Method

- Scientific method is an organized way of using experience and testing ideas in order to expand and refine knowledge.
    - Hypothesis: is a specific statement about behavior or mental processes that is tested through research.
    - Test the hypothesis through controlled methods such as the experiment.
    - Replication: repeating a study to see if the findings hold up over time with different subjects.

Samples and Populations

- Sample
- Population
- Types of Sampling.
    - Random sample:
        - each member of the population has an equal chance of being selected to participate.
    - Stratified sample:
        - selection is made so that identified subgroups in the population are represented proportionately in the sample.
- Volunteer bias:
    - people who volunteer as participants differ systematically from people who do not.

Methods of Observation

- The Case Study.
    - Information collected about individuals and small groups.
    - Anecdotes
    - Compelling portraits but may have factual inaccuracies.

- The Survey.
    - Used to study individuals who cannot be observed in the natural setting or studied scientifically.

- Naturalistic Observation.
    - Observe people in their natural habitats.

Correlation

- Investigates whether one observed behavior or trait is related to (correlated) with another.

- Mathematically expressed as a correlation coefficient; a number the varies between +1.00 and -1.00.

- Correlational studies may suggest but do not prove cause and effect.

Experiments

- Involves Independent and Dependent Variables.
    - Independent variable:
        - manipulated by the experimenters so that the effects of various levels may be determined.
    - Dependent variable:
        - the measured outcome or result.
    - Experimental and Control Groups
        - Experimental groups obtain the treatment.
        - Control groups do not receive the treatment.
- Blind and Double Blind Experiments.
    - Placebo or "sugar pill".
    - Blind.
    - Double blind:

Ethical Issues in Psychological Research and Practice

- Basic standards.
    - Intended to promote individual dignity, human welfare and scientific integrity.
    - Do not undertake research methods that are harmful.

- Research with Humans.
    - Ethics review committees review research according to ethical guidelines.
    - Informed consent: individuals give consent before they can participate in research.
    - Confidentiality is kept.

CONTROVERSY IN PSYCHOLOGY

- Is it ethical for psychologist to deceive research participants about the methods and objectives of their research?

- APA's *Ethical Principles of Psychologists and Code of Conduct* .

Research with Nonhuman Animals

- Psychologists generalize to humans the results of research conducted with animals.

- Animals may be harmed only when there is no alternative and when the researchers believe that the benefits justify the harm.

Critical Thinking, Science, and Pseudoscience.

Pseudoscience: false science.

- Critical thinking: taking nothing for granted. Thoughtfully analyzing and probing questions, statements and arguments of others.

Principles of Critical Thinking

- Be skeptical.

- Examine definitions of terms.

- Examine the assumptions or premises of arguments.

- Be cautious in drawing conclusions from evidence.

- Consider alternative interpretations of research evidence.

- Do not oversimplify.

- Do not overgeneralize.

- Apply critical thinking to all areas of life.

Critical Thinking and Astrology

- Barnum effect.

- Gallup and Newport (1991)
  - one person in four in the U.S. believe in astrology.

- National Science Foundation (2002)
  - 43% of Americans occasionally check their horoscopes
  - though most (60%) reject astrology.

- The "validity" of astrology is confirmed when the astrologer says something positive about the individual.

Chapter 2: Biology and Psychology

Evolution

- Charles Darwin: The Man.
  - Presented "On the Origin of the Species by Natural Selection" in 1859.

Evolution and Evolutionary Psychology

- Theory of Evolution.
  - Natural Selection:
  - Biology serves as the material base for our behaviors, emotions and cognitions.
  - Mutations:
  - differences in individual traits and/or adaptations for survival
- Evolutionary Psychology:
  - Applying adaptation and natural selection to mental processes and behavior.

Heredity

- One's biological structures and processes transmitted from generation to generation.
- Behavioral Genetics:
  - Bridges the sciences of psychology and biology. Concerned with the genetic transmission of traits that give rise to patterns of behaviors.

Heredity: The Nature of Nature

- Molecular Genetics.
- Genes.
- Chromosomes.
- DNA.

Human Genome Project:

- has learned that the sequencing of your DNA consists of about 3 billion DNA sequences.
- Genetic Code:
  - The DNA sequences that "define" each person.
  - Sperm and Egg:
  - Sex Chromosomes:
    - The 23rd pair of chromosomes which determine a person's sex, male or female. X female; Y male.
    - Determined by father.

Kinship Studies

- Attempt to compare traits and behavior patterns in people who are biologically related or unrelated to help determine the role of genetic factors.

Adoption Studies

- Look for similarities between children, their natural and adoptive parents.
  - When children reared by adoptive parents are more similar to their natural parents in a particular trait, strong evidence exists for a genetic role.

Selective Breeding

- Enhances desired physical and behavioral traits.
  - Examples: cattle, chicken, dogs.
  - Tryon rat studies: Bred rats to become "maze dull" and "maze bright".

The Nervous System

- Neurons: the nerve cells of the body
  - Cell Body:
    - contains the nucleus which generates energy
  - Dendrites:
    - receive incoming messages from adjourning cells (roots).
  - Axon:
    - carry messages away from the cell body (trunk).
  - Terminals (terminal buttons):
    - bulb shaped structure at the end of the axon.
  - Myelin:
    - fatty substance around axons that facilitate conduction.
  - Glial cells:
    - remove dead neurons and waste products from the nervous system.

The Neural Impulse

- A message traveling along the neuron; between 2 and 225 miles an hour.
- An Electrochemical Voyage.
  - Neuron resting potential:
    - -70 millivolts (negative charge).
  - Depolarized:
    - action of the cell while it becomes positively charged.
  - Action potential:
    - positively charged neuron returning to the resting state of being negatively charged. The "message" is sent.

Firing

- neurons attempt to transmit messages to other neurons, muscles or glands.
  - Threshold:

- All or None Principle:
- Refractory Period:
- Synapse:

Neurotransmitters: The Chemical Keys to Communication

- Synaptic Vesicles:
  - sacs in the axon terminals which contain neurotransmitters.

- Neurotransmitters:
  - the chemical keys to communication which influence the receiving neuron
  - Receptor Site:
    - specifically tailored site on the receiving neuron where the chemical key (neurotransmitter) fits.
  - Reuptake:
    - reabsorption of neurotransmitters by the sending neuron.
  - Excitatory:
    - neurotransmitter influence on the receiving cell causing it to fire.
  - Inhibitory:
    - neurotransmitter influence on the receiving cell preventing it from firing.

Types of Neurotransmitters

- Acetylcholine (ACh):

- Dopamine:

- Norepinephrine:

- Serotonin:

- Gamma-aminobutyric acid (GABA):

- Endorphins:

The Parts of the Nervous System

- Nerve:
  - a bundle of axons.
- Central Nervous System:
  - brain and spinal cord.
- Peripheral Nervous System:
  - afferent and efferent neurons which transmit messages from the brain or spinal cord to muscles and glands.

The Peripheral Nervous System

- Somatic Nervous System:
  - afferent and efferent neurons that transmit sights, sounds, smells, temperature, body positions, etc.
  - Purposeful body movements.
- Autonomic Nervous System:
  - "Automatic" regulates the glands and internal organ muscles; heartbeat, respiration, digestion, dilation of

9

the pupils, etc.

- Sympathetic Division:
  - active during processes that involve spending body energy; fight or flight.
- Parasympathetic Division:
  - active during processes that replenish reserves of energy.

The Central Nervous System

- Spinal Cord: column of nerves transmits messages from sensory receptors to the brain and from the brain to muscles and glands throughout the body
  - Spinal Reflexes: unlearned response to a stimulus that may involve only two neurons: afferent and efferent.
  - Interneuron: a third neuron that transmits the neural impulse from the sensory neuron through the spinal cord to the motor neuron.
  - Gray Matter: non-myelinated neurons; found in brain and spinal cord.
  - White Matter: myelinated neurons; found in brain and spinal cord.

The Brain: The Star of the Nervous System

- Gender Differences
  - Size
    - Men 15% larger (related to body size difference)
  - How well connected
    - Women metabolize more glucose and use more of their brains

Seeing the Brain Through the Eyes of the Psychologist

- Accidents.
  - provide unplanned, uncontrolled opportunities of studying the brain (see Phineas Gage).
- Experimenting with the Brain.
  - Lesioning: damaging part of the brain.
- The Electroencephalograph (EEG).
  - EEG detects minute amounts of electrical activity in the brain.
- Brain Imaging Techniques.

CAT (computerized axial tomograph)

- A scan which passes a narrow X-ray beam through the head and measures brain structures.
- Generates a three dimensional image of the brain.
- Reveals deformities in shape and structure that are connected with blood clots, tumors, and other health problems.

MRI (magnetic reasoning imaging)

- Person lies in a powerful magnetic field and is exposed to radio waves that cause parts of the brain to emit signals.

- Relies on subtle shifts in blood flow.

- MRI has shown people with schizophrenia have smaller prefrontal regions but larger ventricles.

PET (positron emission tomography)

- computer generated image of the activity of parts of the brain by tracing the amount of glucose used.

Voyage Through the Brain

Hindbrain: where the spinal cord meets the brain. Contains three structures.
- Medulla:
  - regulates vital functions such as heart rate, blood pressure, and respiration.
- Pons:
  - transmits information about body movements and is involved in functions related to attention, sleep/alertness and respiration.
- Cerebellum:
  - involved in maintaining balance and controlling motor behavior.
- Reticular Activating System (RAS):
  - vital in the functions of attention, sleep and arousal.

Forebrain

- forward most part of the brain containing thalamus, hypothalamus, limbic system and the cerebrum.

- Thalamus:
  - relay station for sensory stimulation.

- Hypothalamus:
  - vital for body temperature regulation, concentration of fluids, storage of nutrients, aspects of motivation and emotion.

- Limbic System:
  - Includes the amygdala, hippocampus, and parts of the hypothalamus.
  - Involved in memory, emotion and in the drives of hunger, sex and aggression.
  - Amygdala:
    - connected with aggression, fear response, and vigilance.

- Cerebrum:
  - responsible for thinking and language.

Corpus Callosum

- a bundle of some 200 million nerve fibers connecting the two hemispheres.

The Cerebral Cortex.

- Outer layer of the cerebrum about 1/8 of an inch thick.
- Involved in most bodily activities, sensations, and responses.
  - Frontal Lobe:
    - Contains the motor cortex, which causes our body to move.
  - Parietal Lobe:
    - Contains the somatosensory cortex which receives messages from skin senses all over the body.
  - Temporal Lobe:
    - Contains the auditory area (hearing).
  - Occipital Lobe:
    - Is involved with vision.

Language Functions

- Aphasia: disruption in the ability to understand or produce language.
  - Wernicke's Area:
    - in the temporal lobe responds mainly to auditory information.
  - Wernicke's aphasia:
    - impaired ability to comprehend speech and to think of the proper words to express.
  - Broca's area:
    - processes information and sends it to the motor cortex.
  - Broca's aphasia:
    - Damage to this area results; people can understand language but will speak slowly in simple sentences.

Left Brain, Right Brain

- Left Brain, Right Brain.
  - Left brain:
    - primarily logical and intellectual.
  - Right brain:
    - primarily intuitive, creative, and emotional.
- At best this is exaggerated.
- The hemispheres do not act independently as they are connected by the corpus callosum.

Handedness

- Is It Gauche or Sinister to Be Left Handed?
  - Lefties: 8-10% of people are left handed; more common in males.
    - Has been connected with language problems, dyslexia, stuttering, migraine headaches, allergies, schizophrenia.

- On the other side being left handed is associated with artists, musicians, and mathematicians.

Split Brain Experiments

- Some people with epilepsy have split brain operations in which much of their corpus callosum is severed.

- Each hemisphere has a mind of it's own.
  - One patient described a situation he encountered, as one hemisphere liking reading and other not.
  - If he shifted the book from his right hand to his left, his left hand would put the book down.

The Endocrine System: Chemicals in the Bloodstream.
Glands: secrete hormones.
  - Two types:
    - With ducts (saliva, sweat, tears).
    - Without ducts (released into the blood stream).

- Pituitary Gland:
  - implicated in growth.
  - sometimes referred to as the Master Gland as it influences other glands in the endocrine system.

Types of Hormones

- Growth Hormone.

- Prolactin.

- Antidiuretic Hormone (ADH).

- Oxytocin.

- Melatonin.

- Thyroxin.

- Adrenal glands.

- Testosterone: produced by the testes and in small amounts by the ovaries.
  - Considered to be the male sex hormone as it aids in the development of male sex organs.
  - During puberty the release of testosterone promotes the development of primary and secondary sex characteristics.
  - Primary sex characteristics:
    - those characteristics involved in reproduction: increased penis size, sperm producing ability of the testes.
  - Secondary sex characteristics:
    - Not directly related to reproduction: presence of a beard, deeper voice.

- Estrogen and Progesterone: produced by the ovaries and in small amounts by the testes.
  - Fosters female reproductive capacity and secondary sex characteristics.
  - The levels of estrogen and progesterone vary and regulate the woman's menstrual cycle.

Steroids, Behavior and Mental Processes

- Anabolic (synthetic) steroids are used with growth hormone to enhance
  - Athletic prowess
  - Self-confidence
  - Aggressiveness
  - Memory functioning

- Linked liver damage and other health problems

- Estrogen affects women's perceptions of who is attractive
  - Prefer feminized mail faces during most phases of menstrual cycle

Premenstrual Syndrome (PMS)

- 3 out of 4 women report having some psychological and physical problems.

- However only 1 in 10 has symptoms severe enough to impair academic, occupational, or social functioning.

- PMS may be a complex interaction between ovarian hormones and neurotransmitters.

- Once seen as something a woman must tolerate, today there are many treatment options (diet, exercise, hormone treatments).

How to Handle Menstrual Discomfort

- Don't blame yourself.

- Keep track of your menstrual symptoms to help you and your doctor identify patterns.

- Develop strategies for dealing with days on which you experience the most distress.

- Ask yourself whether you harbor self-defeating attitudes that might be compounding distress.

- See a doctor about your symptoms.

- Develop nutritious eating habits.

- If you feel bloated, eat smaller meals.

- Vigorous exercise.

- Check with your doctor about herbal, vitamin and mineral supplements.

- Ibuprofen and other medications available over the counter may be helpful for cramping.

- Menstruation is triggered by a sharp drop off in sex hormones.

- Remember that menstrual problems are time limited.

Chapter 3: The Voyage Through the Lifespan

Prenatal Development

- Germinal stage:
  - the period from conception to implantation. Also known as the "period of the ovum".

- Embryonic stage:
  - the prenatal period of development from implantation until about the eighth week of development.
  - XY or XX
  - Amniotic sac
    - The embryo is suspended within this protective sac.
  - Umbilical cord:
    - connects the embryo to the placenta.

- Fetal stage:
  - the period of development beginning in the third month until birth.

Physical Development in Childhood

- Reflexes:
  - Simple unlearned, stereotypical responses elicited by specific stimuli.
  - Essential to survival
  - Do not involve higher brain functions.
  - Examples include:
    - Rooting:
    - Withdrawal:
    - Moro:
    - Babinski:

Perceptual Development in Childhood

- Fixation time:
  - the amount of time spent looking at one stimulus instead of another. 2-month old infants prefer stimuli that resemble a human face.

- Visual Cliff experiments:
  - 6-8 month old infants develop depth perception and avoid crawling off the "cliff".

- 3-day old infants prefer to hear their mother's voice to those of other women.

- Shortly after birth infants can discriminate tastes and distinguish tastes .

CONTROVERSY IN PSYCHOLOGY
   Is Development Continuous of Discontinuous?
   - Psychologists disagree more strongly on whether aspects of development occur in stages.
   - Piaget and Freud both believed discontinuous.

xx - girl

xy - boy

Jean Piaget's Cognitive-Developmental Theory

- Piaget hypothesized that children's cognitive processes develop in an orderly sequence of stages.
    - Assimilation and Accommodation
        - Assimilation
        - Scheme
        - Accommodation

- Sensorimotor Stage
    - The newborn is capable of assimilation.
    - By about 8-12 months of age the infant realizes that objects that are removed from sight still exist.
    - This is called object permanence

- The Preoperational Stage
    - Characterized by the use of words and symbols to represent objects and relationships among them.
    - Egocentrism
    - Animism
    - Artificialism
    - Conservation
    - Objective Responsibility

- The Concrete Operational Stage
    - Children ages 7-12; show the beginnings of the capacity for adult logic.
    - Children typically do better with tangible (concrete) rather than abstract ideas.
    - Children become subjective in their moral judgments, less egocentric.
    - Reversibility

Evaluation of Piaget
- He may have underestimated children's abilities.
- Cognitive events may happen more continuously.
- Little variation appears in sequence.

Vygotsky

- Vygotsky was not a stage theorist.

- His theory focuses on transmission of information and cognitive skills from generation to generation (processes in teacher/learner relationship).

- Key concepts of his theory.
    - Zone of proximal development (ZPD)
    - Scaffolding

- Zone of Proximal Development
    - Refers to range of tasks that child can carry out with another's help.
    - Outer speech becomes inner speech.

- Cognitive Scaffolding
    - Refers to temporary support by parent/teacher to child learning to perform a task

16

- Once task "clicks" then "scaffold" not needed.

Kohlberg's Theory of Moral Development
- Kohlberg proposed that one must pay attention more to one's own conscience than to law and authority figures in determining what is right and wrong.
- Proposed that moral reasoning follows a specific sequence.
  - Preconventional
  - Conventional
  - Postconventional

- The Preconventional Level
  - Applies to most children through the age of 9.
    - Stage 1 -Obedience and punishment
    - Stage 2 -Good behavior allows people to satisfy needs of self and others.

- The Conventional Level
  - Moral reasoning is judged by conformity to conventional standards of right and wrong.
    - Stage 3: moral behavior meets the expectations of others.
    - Stage 4: moral judgments based on rules that maintain social order.

- The Postconventional Level
  - Moral reasoning is more complex and focuses on dilemmas in which individual needs are pitted against the need to maintain social order and on personal conscience.

Social and Emotional Development in Childhood

- Erik Erikson's Stages of Psychosocial Development
  - First stage: Trust versus Mistrust.
  - Second stage: Autonomy versus Shame and guilt
  - Third stage: Industry versus inferiority.

- Attachment
  - is an emotional tie that is formed between one person and another specific individual.

- Patterns of Attachment
  - Secure attachment:
  - Avoidant attachment
  - Ambivalent/resistant attachment:

- Three Stages of Attachment
  - Initial-Preattachment Phase (Birth to 3 months):
    - Characterized by indiscriminant attachment.
  - Attachment-in-the-Making Phase (3-4 months of age):
    - Characterized by preference for familiar figures.
    - Specific attachment begins to form about 4 months.
  - Clear-Cut-Attachment Phase (6-7 months):
    - Characterized by intensified dependence on the

primary caregiver.

- Theories of Attachment
  - Behaviorists believe that attachment is learned through experience.
  - Harry Harlow suggests that skin contact may be more important than learning experiences.
  - Konrad Lorenz (ethologist) noted that attachment is an instinct.

- Parenting styles
  - Parental behavior researched by Baumrind focused on four aspects of parental behavior:
    - 1) strictness,
    - 2) demands for a child to achieve intellectual, emotional and social maturity,
    - 3) communication ability, and
    - 4) warmth and involvement.
  - Based on research in this area four parenting styles have been proposed: Authoritative, Authoritarian, Permissive, Uninvolved:

- Child Abuse
  - Contributors to child abuse include:
    - Stress
    - History of child abuse
    - Acceptance of violence as a coping mechanism
    - Failure to attach to children
    - Substance abuse
    - Rigid attitudes toward child rearing
    - Unemployment, and low socioeconomic status
  - Children who are abused are likely to develop personal and social problems, and psychological disorders.
  - There is not an identifiable syndrome for children who have been sexually abused, though they are more likely to develop physical and psychological health problems.
  - Why does abuse run in families?
    - Parents serve as role models.
    - Children adopt their parent's strict philosophies.
    - Abuse creates feelings of hostility that are expressed against others.

Physical Development in Adolescence

- Neither children nor adults; a period of transition.

- Physical Development
  - Growth spurts last for 2-3 years. Grow 8-12 inches.
  - Puberty:
    - a period during which the body becomes sexually mature.

Cognitive Development in Adolescence

- Piaget's stage of Formal Operations (about 11 or 12).
    - Abstract thought
    - Adolescent Egocentrism
        - Press for acceptance of their logic without recognizing exceptions; egocentric thought
        - Imaginary Audience:
        - Personal Fable:
- Kohlberg's Postconventional Level of Moral Reasoning
    - Highest level is based on person's own moral standards.
        - Stage 5: legalistic orientation; law is good for society.
        - Stage 6: moral reasoning demands adherence to supposed universal ethics.
    - Conscience is the highest moral authority.

CONTROVERSY IN PSYCHOLOGY
Are there gender differences in moral development?

- Using the Heinz dilemma boys show higher levels of moral development than girls.
- Carol Gilligan proposes that this is due to different socialization patterns for boys and girls not differences in morality.
- Girls are socialized to focus on the needs of others and forgo simplistic judgments of right and wrong. Boys make judgments based on logic.

Social and Emotional Development in Adolescence

- Storm and Stress.
    - Need to take into account individual differences and cultural variations.
    - 72% of all deaths among people aged 10-24 years result from:
        - motor vehicle crashes
        - homicide
        - suicide
        - other unintentional injuries
    - Research evidence suggests that hormonal changes affect activity levels but sociocultural influences have a relatively greater impact.
- Adolescents strive for independence which often leads to:
    - Fighting with parents
    - Withdrawal from family life; though most adolescents continue to feel love, respect and loyalty toward their parents.
    - Adolescents who feel close to their parents show:
        - Greater self reliance
        - Independence
        - Fare better in school

- Have fewer adjustment problems
- Ego Identity Versus Role Diffusion: Who Am I?
  - The fifth stage of Erikson's theory.
  - Ego Identity:
    - a firm sense of who one is and what one stands for.
    - If this isn't accomplished then role diffusion is experienced.
- Adolescent Sexuality
  - Problems:
    - Adolescents often misunderstand reproduction and contraception.
    - Top reason for engaging in sex is peer pressure.
    - Pregnancies are more likely to be characterized by medical complications, prolonged labor, premature births.
    - Teen mothers are less likely to graduate from high school, have a lower standard of living, and have a greater need for public assistance.
  - The final decade of the 20th century saw a decline in teenage pregnancy due to increased use of contraception and educational campaigns.

Physical Development in Adulthood

- Young adulthood characteristics:
  - Height of sensory sharpness, strength, reaction time, and cardiovascular fitness.
  - Sexually, most people are easily aroused and able to perform.
- Middle adulthood characteristics:
  - Diminished strength, coordination, and stamina but it is minor.
  - Can still maintain excellent cardiorespiratory condition.
  - Menopause: final phase of the climacteric.
- Late adulthood characteristics:
  - Increased numbers of people in this age range.
  - Increased brittleness in the bones.
  - See and hear less acutely.
  - Reaction time diminishes.
  - Immune system functions less efficiently.
- Theories of Aging
  - Programmed Senescence:
  - Wear and Tear Theory:
- Hakim (1998) researched the value of exercise and found walking at least two miles a day helps.

Cognitive Development in Adulthood

- Characteristics include: creativity, memory functioning and intelligence all of which are at their height in adulthood.

- Memory function does decline with age.

- People tend to retain their verbal skills and general knowledge into advanced age.

- Crystallized versus Fluid Intelligence.

Cognitive Development in Adulthood

- Alzheimer's Disease.
  - It is a disease, not a normal part of aging.
  - Seems to be a result of reduced levels of acetylcholine (ACh) and the build up of sticky plaque on the brain.

Social and Emotional Development in Adulthood

- Characteristics include social and emotional development being the most fluid in adulthood.

- Psychologically adults are healthier as they advance from adolescence.

- Adults are more productive and have better interpersonal relationships.

- Young Adulthood:
  - adults establish themselves as independent members of society.
    - Fueled by ambition; wanting to advance their careers.
    - Dream:
      - the drive to become someone, to leave their mark on history; a tentative blueprint for their life.
    - Erikson proposed that young adults enter a stage of intimacy versus isolation.
      - This is marked by the establishment of intimate relationships.
    - Levinson labeled this time period as the "age-30 transition. Young adults ask themselves, "Where am I going?" and "Why am I doing this?".

- Middle Adulthood:
  - key changes in social and emotional development take place.

- Generativity versus stagnation.
  - Generativity is doing things that we believe are worthwhile which enhances self-esteem and helps shape a new generation.
  - Stagnation is "treading water" and has powerful destructive effects on self esteem.

- Levinson called this time period "midlife transition".
  - There is a shift in psychological perspective as people begin to think of how many years they have left.

- Women may undergo a midlife transition a number of years earlier than men do.
  - Winding down the biological clock; the ability to conceive and bear children.

- Levinson proposed that this period may trigger for some, a midlife crisis.

CONTROVERSY IN PSYCHOLOGY
Do Women Experience an Empty Nest Syndrome?

- Empty nest syndrome
  - characterized by profound sense of loss when the youngest child leaves.

- Many mothers report increased marital satisfaction and greater mellowness, self confidence and stability.

- Stewart (1998) developed a scale to assess four personality variables:
  - Identity certainty
  - Confident power
  - Generativity: similar to Erikson's.
  - Awareness of aging.
  - They found that middle age frees many women from gender-related, traditional, roles.

- Late Adulthood
  - Erikson proposed a stage of ego integrity versus despair.
  - Ego integrity derives from wisdom; expert knowledge, balance, and excellence.

- Successful Aging.
  - Most people in their 70s report general satisfaction with lives.
  - Three factors are connected with subjective well-being (Pinquart & Sorensen, 2000):
    - Socioeconomic status.
    - Social network.
    - Competence.

- Volz (2000) proposes three components for successful aging:
  - Reshaping one's life to concentrate on what one finds to be important and meaningful.
  - A positive outlook.
  - Self challenge.

On Death and Dying

- Kubler-Ross proposed five stages of dying:
  - Denial.
  - Anger.
  - Bargaining.
  - Depression.
  - Final acceptance.

Life Connections: Day Care

- A great majority of mothers are now in the workforce.
- How does day care affect the bonds of attachment?
- How does day care influence social and cognitive development?

- Statistics show that:
  - Nature of the family-child interactions had a greater impact than child care.
  - Some aggressiveness may be children adapting responses to limited resources.
- Most of the problems that were observed were not that serious.

Finding day care you can live with

- Does the day care have a license?
- How many children are cared for by the day care center?
- How were the caregivers hired?
- Is the environment child proofed and secure?
- When are meals served?
- Is it possible to meet the caregivers?
- With what children will your child interact and play?
- Does the center seem to have an enriching environment?
- Are there facilities and objects like swings, tricycles, etc.?
- Does the center's schedule coincide with your needs?
- Is the center location convenient for you?
- Are parents permitted to visit unannounced?
- Do you like the overall environment?

Chapter 4: Sensation and Perception

Sensation and Perception

- Sensation:
  - is the stimulation of sensory receptors and the transmission of sensory information to the central nervous system.

- Perception:
  - is an active process in which sensations are organized and interpreted to form an inner representation of the world.

- Five Senses:

Psychophysics

- Focuses on ways in which we translate physical events such as light and sounds into psychological experiences.

Absolute Threshold

- refers to the weakest amount of a stimulus that a person can distinguish from no stimulus at all 50% of the time.
  - Examples include:
    - Vision: candle flame viewed from about 30 miles on a clear, dark night.
    - Hearing: a watch ticking from about 20 feet away in a quiet room.
    - Taste: 1 teaspoon of sugar dissolved in 2 gallons of water.
    - Smell: about one drop of perfume diffused throughout a small house (1 part in 500 million).
    - Touch: the pressure of the wing of a fly falling on a cheek from a distance of about 0.4 inch.

Difference Threshold

- the minimum difference in magnitude of two stimuli required to tell them apart 50% of the time.

- Similar to the just noticeable difference (jnd).
  - Weber found that for:
    - Light the fraction is $1/60^{th}$.
    - Weight the fraction is $1/53^{rd}$.
    - Constant pitch the fraction is 1/333.

Signal-Detection Theory

- Considers the human aspects of sensation, and perception

- Assumes that the relationship between a physical stimulus and a sensory response is not just mechanical.

- Other factors include:
  - Training (learning).
  - Motivation (desire to perceive).

— Psychological states such as fatigue or alertness.

Feature Detectors in the Brain

- Brain cells that respond to different aspects of features of a scene (e.g. angles, vertical, horizontal).

Sensory Adaptation

- The sensory process of adjustment.
  - Sensitization (Positive adaptation)
    - Becoming more sensitive to stimulation.
  - Desensitization (Negative adaptation)
    - Becoming less sensitive to stimulation.

Vision

- More than half of our brain's cerebral cortex is devoted to visual functions.
- Light
  - All forms of electromagnetic energy moves in waves.
  - Sir Isaac Newton discovered the prism that could break light into different colors. Colors of the spectrum include:
    - Red, orange, yellow, green, blue, indigo, violet (Roy G. Biv)

The Eye

- Light first passes through the transparent cornea.
- The amount of light that is allowed to enter is controlled by the muscle called the iris (the colored part of the eye).
- The actual opening in the iris is called the pupil.
- The lens adjusts or accommodates to the image by changing its thickness. The thickness permits a clear image of the object to be projected onto the retina.
- The retina
- Rods and Cones

Problems with the Rods and Cones
  - Nearsighted:
  - Farsighted:
  - Presbyopia

Light Adaptation

- Dark adaptation:
  - the process of adjusting to lower lighting conditions.
- Light adaptation
  - Adapting to brighter lighting takes place much more rapidly.

Color Vision

- The wavelength of light determines its color or hue.

- The value of color is its degree of lightness or darkness.

- Saturation refers to how intense a color appears.

- Warm and Cold Colors.
    - Colors on the green-blue side of the color wheel are considered to be cool in temperature.
    - Colors on the yellow-red side are considered to be warm.

- Complementary Colors.
    - The colors across from one another on the color wheel are complementary.

- Afterimages.
    - Persistent sensations of color are followed by perception of the complimentary color when the first color is removed.

- Theories of color vision
    - Our ability to perceive color depends on the eye's transmission of different messages to the brain when lights with different wavelengths stimulate the cones in the retina.

CONTROVERSY IN PSYCHOLOGY:
When Light With Different Wavelengths Stimulate The Retina

Trichromatic Theory.
    - Young found that he could create any color from the visible spectrum by varying the intensities of three lights: red, green, and blue-violet.

- Opponent-Process theory.
    - Hering proposed that there are three types of color receptors but they don't respond just to red, green and blue-violet.

- Research suggests that each theory of color vision is partially correct.
    - The cones may be as Helmholtz claimed.
    - The transmission of the signals to the brain are as Hering proposed.

Color Blindness

- If you can discriminate among the colors of the visible spectrum, you have normal color vision and are labeled a trichromat.

- People who are totally color blind are called monochromats.

- Partially color-blind people are called dichromats.

Visual Perception

- Visual perception
    - is the process by which we organize or make sense of the sensory impressions caused by the light that strikes our eyes.

- Gestalt psychologists refer to closure as being

– the integration of disconnected pieces of information into a meaningful whole, or

Perceptual Organization

- Gestalt psychologists are interested in the way we integrate bits and pieces of sensory stimulation into meaningful wholes.

- Figure-Ground Perception.
  - When figure-ground relationships are ambiguous, or capable of being interpreted in various ways, our perceptions tend to be unstable, shifting back and forth.

- Other Gestalt Rules for Organization:
  - Proximity
  - Similarity
  - Continuity
  - Common Fate

- Top-Down Versus Bottom-Up Processing.
  - Top-Down Processing
    - Use the larger pattern to guide subordinate tasks.
  - Bottom-Up processing
    - Begin with bits and pieces of information and become aware of the pattern.

Perception of Motion

- Visual perception of movement is based on change of position relative to other objects.

- Types of apparent movement (illusions of movement).
  - The Autokinetic Effect
  - Stoboscopic Motion
  - The Phi Phenomenon

Depth Perception

- Monocular Cues: cues that can be perceived by one eye.
  - Perspective.
  - Relative size.
  - Clearness of an object.
  - Interposition.
  - Shadows.
  - Texture Gradient.
  - Motion Parallax.

- Binocular Cues: cues that can be perceived by both eyes.
  - Retinal disparity.
  - Convergence.

Perceptual Constancies

- Size constancy:
  - Allows us to perceive objects to be the same size even when viewed from different distances.

- Color constancy:
  - The tendency to perceive objects as retaining their color even though lighting conditions may alter their

appearance.
- Brightness constancy:
  - similar to color constancy.
- Shape constancy:
  - The tendency to perceive objects as maintaining their shape.

Visual Illusions: Is Seeing Believing?
The Hering-Helmholtz and Muller-Lyer.
  - These illusions work because of our life experience.
    - Lifelong use of perceptual cues.
    - Experience with perspectives.
  - The Ponzo illusions seems to work because of size constancy.

Hearing

- Sound or auditory stimulation, travels through the air like waves.
- Pitch and Loudness
  - Pitch of a sound is determined by
    - its frequency, or the number of cycles per second as expressed in the unit hertz (Hz).
  - Loudness of a sound roughly corresponds
    - to the height or amplitude of sound.

The Ear

  The outer ear is shaped to funnel sound waves to the eardrum.
- The middle ear functions as an amplifier.
  - The stirrup is attached to another vibrating membrane (the oval window) which transmits vibrations to the cochlea.
  - The cochlea is a snail shaped structure that contains membranes.
  - One of these membranes is the basilar membrane.
  - Attached to the basilar membrane is the command post of hearing (organ of Corti).
  - Here there are receptor cells called hair cells.
  - Hair cells dance in response to basilar membrane vibrations.
  - Their movements generate neural impulses which are sent to the brain via the auditory nerve.
  - Auditory input is then projected onto the hearing areas of the temporal lobes of the cerebral cortex

Locating Sounds

- A sound that is louder in the right ear is perceived as coming from the right.
- Both loudness and the sequence in which the sounds reach the ears provide directional cues.
- Perception of Loudness and Pitch.
  - The loudness and pitch of sounds appear to be related
    - to the number of receptor neurons on the organ of Corti that fire, and

- how often they fire.
- Psychologists generally agree that sounds are perceived as louder when more of these sensory neurons fire.

CONTROVERSY IN PSYCHOLOGY: Explaining Fluctuations in Hearing

- Place theory.
- Frequency theory.
- The volley principle.

Deafness

- More than 1 in 10 Americans has a hearing impairment, and 1 in 100 cannot hear at all.
- Two major types of deafness are conductive and sensorineural deafness.
  - Conductive deafness.
  - Sensorineural deafness.

The Chemical Senses

- Smell
  - If you did not have a sense of smell an onion and an apple would taste the same to you.
  - Humans can detect the odor of 1 one-millionth of a milligram of vanilla in a liter of air.
  - An odor is a sample of the substance being sensed.
  - The sense of smell adapts rapidly to odors such that we lose awareness of them.

- Taste
  - Four primary taste qualities: sweet, sour, salty, and bitter.
  - Food flavor depends on its odor, texture, temperature as well as taste.
  - Taste cells are receptor neurons located on taste buds.

The Skin Senses

- The skin senses include touch, pressure, warmth, cold, and pain.
- Touch and Pressure:
  - Active touching involves reception of information concerning not only touch per se but also pressure, temperature, and feedback from the muscles involved in movements of our hands.
  - Psychophysicists use methods such as the two-point threshold to assess sensitivity to pressure.
- Temperature
  - The receptors for temperature are neurons located just beneath the skin.

Kinesthesis and the Vestibular Sense.

- Kinesthesis:
    - the sense that informs you about the position and motion of parts of the body.

- The Vestibular Sense
    - Your vestibular sense tells you whether you are upright.

Sensation and Perception and Virtual Reality

- Virtual reality is perception of events fed directly into senses via electronic technology

Virtual Reality

- Virtual Room
    - Can transform ways that people gather and interact.

- Cybersex: What are psychological implications?
    - Deterioration of sense of self?
    - Decreased sensitivity to real life romantic partners?
    - Would virtual sex be adultery?

Extrasensory Perception

- Hard research does not support the existence of ESP.
    - Nonetheless 60% of Americans believe that some people have psychic powers or ESP.

- Examples of ESP phenomena:
    - Precognition.
    - Psychokinesis.
    - Telepathy.
    - Clairvoyance.
    - Psi communication.

Research in Extrasensory Perception

- Rhine studied ESP for several decades with the conclusion that some people might have some degree of ESP.
    - Ganzfeld Procedure.
    - File drawer problem.

- People who have demonstrated ESP with one researcher have failed to do so with another researcher.

- Not one person has emerged who can reliably show psi communication from one occasion to another and from one researcher to another.

LIFE CONNECTIONS:
Pain, Pain, Go Away-Don't Come Again Another Day.
Pain means that something is wrong in the body.
    - Pain is adaptive.
    - There are no nerve endings for pain in the brain.
    - Postaglandins (substance P) facilitate transmission of the pain message to the brain and heighten circulation

30

to the injured area.
- Other aspects influence pain:
- Visual and other sensory inputs tell us what is happening and influence the cognitive interpretation of the situation.

- Phantom Limb Pain.
  - Seems to involve activation of nerves in the stump of the missing limb.

- Gate Theory.
  - The nervous system can process only a limited amount of stimulation at a time.

- Acupuncture.
  - Research has shown that acupuncture stimulates nerves that reach the hypothalamus and may also result in the release of endorphins.

- Modern Psychological Methods for Coping with Pain.
  - The primary treatment has been chemical; pain-killing drugs.
  - Accurate Information.
  - Distraction and Fantasy.
  - Hypnosis has been used to reduce chronic pain, as an anesthetic in dentistry, childbirth, even in some forms of surgery.

- Modern Psychological Methods for Coping with Pain.
  - Relaxation Training and Biofeedback.
  - Coping with Irrational Beliefs.
  - Other methods.
    - Sense of commitment.
    - Supportive social networks help as well.

Chapter 5: Consciousness

The Many Meanings of Consciousness?

- Examples of constructs associated with consciousness include:
  - sensory awareness,
  - selective attention,
  - direct inner awareness,
  - personal unity, and
  - a waking state.

Consciousness as Sensory Awareness

- When we are aware of the environment, we are conscious of it.
  - Vision allows us to see or be conscious of the snow.
  - Hearing allows us to hear or be conscious of a concert.

Selective Aspect of Attention

- Selective attention
  - Focusing on one stimulus out of many stimuli.
  - Learning which stimuli must be attended to and which can be safely ignored allows us to adapt to our environment.

Direct Inner Awareness

- An individual's awareness of personal thoughts, images, emotions, and memories.

- Levels of consciousness (Freud):
  - Conscious
  - Preconscious
  - Unconscious.

- Nonconscious bodily processes which cannot be experienced through our sensory awareness or direct inner awareness.

Personal Unity

- As we get older, it is important for us to be individuals, different from other people.

- Our impressions, thoughts and feelings combine to make up our continuing self in a changing world.

- In this usage, consciousness is "self".

Waking State
Consciousness also applies to our waking state compared to sleep
  - Distorted perceptions of reality called "altered states of consciousness".

Sleep and Dreams

- Stage 1
  - Brain waves slow down further to 6-8 cycles/sec (theta waves).
  - Stage 1 lasts 30-40 min.

- Stage 2:
  - Brain waves slow to 4-7 cycles/sec
  - Sleep spindles or brief bursts of brain activity 12-16 cycles/sec occur.

- Stages 3 and 4:
  - Brain waves slow to 1-3 cycles/sec (delta waves) during stage 3, these same delta waves slow down to 0.5-2 cycles/sec in stage 4.
  - Difficult to wake a person in stage 4 sleep.

Awakening from Sleep

- We begin the journey back through the stages (from 4 to 1) until we enter REM (rapid eye movement) sleep.

- Brain waves resemble rapid, low amplitude brain waves of Stage 1.

- Often called paradoxical sleep because EEG patterns look like an awake person's waves.

- Difficult to awaken a person in REM.

- If you wake a person, 80% of the time he or she will report having been dreaming.

- Dreaming in NREM occurs but is less frequent (20%).

Functions of Sleep

There are still many questions about why we sleep.

- Lack of sleep for several nights leads to impairments in:
  - Attention,
  - learning, and
  - memory.

- The amount of sleep we need is related to
  - genetics,
  - stress, and
  - age.

- Sleep, Learning, and Memory
  - Being REM deprived interferes with memory.
  - Once REM deprived, person can catch-up REM sleep in later sleep periods.

Dreams: What is the Stuff of Dreams?

- Dreams involve imagery in the absence of external stimulation and usually occur during REM sleep.

- Theories on Dream Content
  - Dreams involve activities or content from day.
  - Freud theorized that dreams reflect unconscious wishes and urges.

- Activation synthesis model suggests that ACh and the pons stimulate responses that lead to dreaming.
- PET scans show that the brain's frontal lobes are shut down during sleep.
- Memories are replayed and consolidated during sleep.
- Dreams are the by-products of brain testing.

Sleep Disorders - Insomnia

- National Sleep Foundation (2000b) reports that as many as 58% of American adults are affected by insomnia in a given year.
- Factors contributing to insomnia include:
  - Stress
  - Pain
  - Children
  - Partner's snoring
  - Pauses in partner's breathing
- Individuals with insomnia may increase its severity by attempting to force sleep.

Sleep Disorders - Narcolepsy

- Sudden and irresistibly falling asleep.
- Typically lasts 15 minutes.
- May be accompanied by sleep paralysis
- Thought to be a disorder of REM sleep

Sleep Disorders - Apnea

- People stop breathing numerous times per hour.
- Apnea is associated with obesity and chronic loud snoring.
- May be caused by anatomical deformities that clog air passages and problems in the breathing centers of the brain.

Deep Sleep Disorders

- Because deep sleep disorders (stage 3 or 4) are more common in children, they may reflect an immaturity of the nervous system.
  - Sleep Terrors
  - Bed Wetting
  - Sleep Walking

Daydreams/Fantasies

- Differ from other dreams because they occur while awake.
  - Some think they are a sign of a life that lacks enrichment or enjoyment, but can provide pleasure and allow for contemplation of future possibilities.

Sexual Fantasies

- Research suggests it is "normal" to fantasize about sex.

- Gender differences in sexual fantasies
  - Males fantasize more frequently.
  - Male fantasies are more forceful than females.

Aggressive Fantasies

- Tend to become common in adolescence

- Females experience them, but not as frequently as males.

Altering Consciousness Through Hypnosis

- Hypnosis
  - An altered state of consciousness where people appear highly suggestible

- Began with Franz Mesmer (mesmerize) in the 18th century

- Today hypnosis is used to help people reduce anxiety or overcome fears

- Hypnotic Suggestibility
  - Knowledge of what is expected during trance.
  - Prone to Fantasy
  - Compartmentalize unwanted memories,
  - Want to cooperate with the hypnotist.

- It is extremely unlikely that someone could be hypnotized against their will.

Controversy in Psychology
How do Psychologists Explain Hypnosis?

- Role Theory

- Response Set Theory

- Neodissociation Theory

Altering Consciousness Through Meditation

- Meditation refers to focusing consciousness in order to alter one's relationship to the world.

- Can also refer to the process of suspending thinking and allow the world to fade away.

- Transcendental meditation (TM)

Altering Consciousness through Biofeedback

- Biofeedback is a system that provides information or "feed back" about a bodily function.
  - Once we have this information, we can use it to change body functions once thought to be involuntary (Ex. heart rate).

Altering Consciousness Through Drugs

- Psychoactive drugs can distort perceptions and change mood.

- Substance abuse
  - the repeated use of a substance despite its contribution to social, occupational, psychological, physical problems.
- Dependence
  - more severe than abuse because it is often characterized by:
  - Tolerance: the body's habituation to a substance so that higher dosages are required to achieve similar effects.
  - Withdrawal or abstinence syndromes: noticeable effects when level of usage suddenly drops off.

Causal Factors in Substance Abuse and Dependence

- Reasons people report experimenting with drugs include:
  - curiosity,
  - conformity to peer pressure,
  - parental use,
  - rebelliousness,
  - Escapism, and
  - sensation seeking.
- A CDC survey indicated that teen drug and cigarette use increased over the past decade.
- Psychological views suggest that
  - Expectations about drug effects are powerful predictors of use.
  - Individuals use drugs to self medicate for anxiety and depression.
- Biological views suggest genetic predispositions for drug use.

Depressants: Alcohol

- Relieves anxiety, depression, or loneliness, and lowers inhibitions.
- Larger doses have sedative effect which:
  - Impairs cognitive functioning, slurs speech, and reduces motor coordination.
  - Induces feelings of elation and euphoria.
- Regular drinking leads to dependence.

Controversy in Psychology
Is a Drink a day Good For You?

- Benefits to light drinking include an
  - increase HDL (good cholesterol) and thus decreases risk of cardiovascular disease,
  - less cognitive decline with age, and
  - decreased risk of Alzheimer's disease.
  - However these benefits disappear with heavy drinking.
- Costs associated with heavy drinking include
  - weight gain,

- interference with absorption of vitamins,
- possibility of disorders associated with drinking (cirrhosis of the liver, Wernicke-Korsakoff syndrome),
- cancer and cardiovascular disease,
- birth defects.

- Alcoholics Anonymous (AA) is the most widely used program.

- Other programs include:
  - Cognitive-behavior therapy, and
  - Motivational-enhancement therapy.

- Research is underway using Disulfiram (Antabuse).

Opiates

- Opioids are similar in chemical structure but are synthetically derived.

- Heroin can cause strong euphoric rushes, drowsiness and stupor, alter perceptions of time, and impair judgment.

- Withdrawal can include flu like symptoms, tremors, cramps, chills which alternate with sweating, rapid pulse, high blood pressure, insomnia, vomiting and diarrhea.

- Methadone, a synthetic opioid is used to reduce these withdrawal symptoms during treatment

Barbiturates

- Barbiturates are depressants which
  - Relieve anxiety, tension, and pain.
  - Treat epilepsy, high blood pressure, and insomnia.
  - Rapidly lead to both physiological and psychological dependence.

Stimulants

- Increase activity in the nervous system.

Amphetamines

- Help people remain alert through the night.

- Other names include "speed," "uppers," or "bennies."

- Often abused because of the euphoric rush they provide.

- High doses of amphetamine may cause restlessness, insomnia, loss of appetite, hallucinations, paranoid delusions, and irritability.

- Tolerance develops rapidly.

Cocaine

- Stimulant that produces euphoria, reduces hunger, deadens pain, and bolsters self-confidence.

- Cause both physical and psychological dependence.

Nicotine

- Stimulates discharge of the hormone adrenaline which
  - Enhances memory and attention,
  - Improves performance on simple repetitive tasks,
  - Enhances mood,
  - Helps people relax and reduces stress.
  - Depresses appetite and raises the metabolic rate.

- Nicotine is addictive and is the chemical that causes the physiological dependence to tobacco products.

- Withdrawal symptoms include nervousness, drowsiness, loss of energy, headaches, irregular bowel movements, lightheadedness, insomnia, dizziness, cramps, palpitations, tremors and sweating.

Nicotine-Why Quit?

- Nearly 430,000 Americans die from smoking related illnesses each year (American Lung Association, 2000).

- Every cigarette smoked steals about 7 minutes of a person's life.
  - Hydrocarbons (tars) are what lead to lung cancer.

- Pregnant women who smoke have a higher risk of miscarriage, preterm births, low birth weight babies, and still born babies.

- Passive smoking is related to respiratory illnesses, asthma, and other health problems.

Hallucinogenics

- Produce hallucinations.

- Can also produce relaxation, euphoria, or in some cases panic.

- Example: Marijuana
  - Produced from the Cannabis sativa plant.
  - Used relaxation or to elevate mood.
  - May also produce mild hallucinations.
  - Impairs perceptual-motor coordination, short term memory, and slows learning.
  - Can increase anxiety, confusion, and psychotic reactions.
  - Strong intoxication can produce nausea and vomiting.
  - People can become psychologically dependent and experience withdrawal symptoms.

Controversy in Psychology
Should Marijuana be Used as Medicine?

- Marijuana has been used to:
  - Treat glaucoma
  - Relieve nausea associated with chemotherapy.

- Benefits in using Marijuana include its
  - Reasonably safety,
  - Inexpensive cost,
  - Versatile use.

- Drawbacks from use
  - Marijuana smoke contains more hydrocarbons than tobacco smoke
  - Many questions about potential harm remain. More research is needed.

Other Hallucinogenics

- LSD
  - Produces vivid and colorful hallucinations
  - Flashbacks are termed hallucinogen persisting perception disorder

- Mescaline (derived from peyote cactus)

Life Connections: Getting to Sleep and Elsewhere without Drugs

- Psychological methods to deal with insomnia:
  - Relax
  - Challenge exaggerated fears
  - Don't ruminate in bed
  - Establish a regular routine
  - Try fantasy

Strategies for Gaining and Maintaining Control

- Gaining Control Physically
  - Detoxification

- Gaining Control Mentally
  - Making a public commitment increases success.
  - Replace the urge to do drugs with other strategies.
  - Engage in activities that don't involve drugs.

Chapter 6: Learning

Learning

- Definition:
  - Learning is a relatively permanent change in behavior that arises from practice or experience.
  - According to cognitive psychologists, learning may be a mental change that may not be associated with changes in behavior.

Classical Conditioning

- Classical conditioning is a simple form of associative learning that enables organisms to anticipate events.

- Reflexes:
  - simple automatic responses to stimuli.

- Stimulus:
  - an environmental condition that evokes a response from an organism.

- Pavlov discovered that reflexes can also be learned through association.

CONTROVERSY IN PSYCHOLOGY:
Why did Pavlov's dogs learn to salivate in response to the bell?

- Organisms form associations between stimuli because the stimuli are contiguous – that is they occur at about the same time.

- Cognitive psychologists view classical conditioning as the learning of relationships among events.

- Stimuli and Responses in Classical Conditioning.
  - Unconditioned stimulus (US) is unlearned.
  - When the dogs learned to salivate to the sound of a bell (previously neutral) the bell became the conditioned stimulus (CS) and the salivation in response to the bell is a conditioned response (CR).

- Taste Aversion: Are All Stimuli Created Equal?
  - Taste aversions are examples of classical conditioning.
    - Taste aversions are adaptive to the organism as they motivate them to avoid potentially harmful food.
    - Different than classical conditioning because:
      - Only one association may be required.
      - The US and CS do not have to be contiguous.
  - The Evolution of Taste Aversion.
    - The evolutionary perspective suggests that animals and humans would be biologically predisposed to develop aversions that are

40

adaptive in their environmental settings.

- Extinction and Spontaneous Recovery help us adapt by updating our expectations about the changing environment.
  - Extinction:
    - the process by which a CS lose the ability to elicit CRs because the CS is no longer paired with the US.
- Spontaneous Recovery:
    - recovery of a CR after extinction. A function of the passage of time.
    - Spontaneous recovery, like extinction, is adaptive.
- Generalization and Discrimination.
  - Generalization
    - the tendency for a conditioned response to be evoked by stimuli similar to the stimulus to which the response was conditioned.
  - Discrimination: organisms must learn that:
    - Many stimuli perceived as being similar are functionally different.
    - The organism must respond adaptively to each.
- Higher Order Conditioning
  - In Higher Order Conditioning a previously neutral stimulus comes to serve as a learned or CS after being paired repeatedly with a stimulus that has already become learned.

Applications of Classical Conditioning

- Counterconditioning:
- Flooding and Systematic Desensitization.
- The Bell and Pad Treatment for Bed Wetting.

Operant Conditioning

- Edward L. Thorndike
  - The Law of Effect: a response is strengthened in a particular situation by a reward (stamped in). Punishments stamp out stimulus-response connections.
- Burrhus Frederic Skinner (1904-1990).
  - Historical contributions: Skinner Box, programmed learning, and Walden II.
- Concepts of Reinforcement
  - Organisms learn to do something because of the effects or consequences of that behavior.
  - Operant conditioning is a simple form of learning in which an organism learns to engage in certain behavior because of the effects of that behavior.
- Methods of Operant Conditioning
  - Skinner devised an operant chamber (Skinner Box); a cage for animals used to study operant conditioning.
  - The First Correct Response:

- it matters little how the first response that is reinforced is made (random or guided)
    - People can be verbally guided into the desired response.
- Any stimulus which increases the probability that responses preceding it will be repeated serves as a reinforcer.
    - Positive Reinforcers:
        - increase the probability the behavior will occur when applied.
    - Negative Reinforcers:
        - increase the probability of a behavior when removed.
    - With sufficient reinforcement operants become habits.
    - Immediate reinforcers are more effective than delayed reinforcers.
    - Primary and Secondary Reinforcers.
        - Primary reinforcers are effective because of an organism's biological makeup (e.g. food and water).
        - Secondary reinforcers acquire their value through being associated with established reinforcers. Sometimes called conditioned reinforcers.
- Extinction and Spontaneous Recovery in Operant Conditioning.
    - Extinction occurs as a result of repeated performance of operant behavior without reinforcement.
    - Spontaneous recovery occurs in operant conditioning. The reward returns and the behavior increases.
- Reinforcers Versus Rewards and Punishments.
    - Reinforcers are known by their effects.
    - Rewards and punishments are known by how they feel.
- Results of using punishment:
    - Children are less likely to develop internal moral standards.
    - Physical punishment is connected with poorer parent-child relationships.
    - Physically punished children are more likely to be aggressive toward other children.
    - Physically punished children are more likely to abuse their spouses or their own children.
- Why not use physical punishment:
    - It hurts.
    - Punished individuals may withdraw from situation (family, school, etc.)
    - Children learn the responses that are punished.
    - Psychologists recommend rewarding good behavior or ignoring misbehavior by using time out.
- Discriminative stimuli act as cues by providing information about when an operant will be reinforced.
- Schedules of Reinforcement:
    - Some responses are maintained by means of

continuous reinforcement; reinforcement after every response.
- Partial reinforcement can also maintain behavior.
- Interval Schedules.
  - Fixed Interval.
  - Variable Interval.
- Schedules of Reinforcement:
  - Ratio schedules.
    - Fixed ratio.
    - Variable ratio.
  - Shaping reinforces progressive steps toward the behavioral goal.
    - Reinforce successive approximations of the goal.

Cognitive Factors in Learning

- Cognitive psychologists use concepts such as mental structures, schemas, templates, and information processing.
- Latent Learning:
  - Tolman showed that rats learn about their environment in the absence of reinforcement.
- Observational Learning:
  - Albert Bandura proposed that we can acquire operants by observing the behavior of others.
    - A person who engages in a response to be imitated is a model.
    - Observers are said to be vicariously reinforced.

Applications of Operant Conditioning

- Biofeedback Training: Gaining Bleep Control.
  - enabled people to learn to control autonomic responses in order to attain reinforcement.
    - Important innovation in treatment of health-related problems.
    - Reinforcement is given in the form of information.
- Behavior Modification in the Classroom.
    - Teachers are taught to pay attention to children when they are behaving appropriately.
    - Older children: peer approval is often more powerful.
- Programmed Learning: Step by Step.
  - Method assumes that any complex task can be broken down into a number of small steps.

Contingency Theory.

- Contingency theory:
  - suggests that learning occurs only when the conditioned stimulus provides information about the unconditioned stimulus.
  - Rescorla concluded that the co-appearance of two events cannot in itself explain classical conditioning.

43

LIFE CONNECTIONS: Violence in the media and aggression.

- If a child watches 2 to 4 hours of TV a day, he/she will have seen 8,000 murders and 100,000 acts of violence by the end of elementary school.

- Bandura, Ross and Ross (1963) found that children who had observed the aggressive model showed significantly more aggressive behavior toward the doll themselves.

- Violence is often shown to have only temporary or minimal effects.

- Few TV programs show harmful long-term effects.

- Ways in which depictions of violence contribute to violence:
  - Observational learning.
  - Disinhibition.
  - Increased emotional arousal.
  - Priming of aggressive thoughts and memories.
  - Habituation.
  - Assumption that violence is acceptable.
  - Decreases the likelihood that one will take action on behalf of a victim.
  - May lead to real-life violence.

- There is no simple one-to-one connection between media violence and violence in real life.

- Family constellations may also contribute:
  - Parental substance abuse.
  - Paternal physical punishments.
  - Single motherhood.
  - Parental rejection.

- Teaching Children Not to Imitate Media Violence.
  - Children who watch violent shows act less aggressively when they are informed that:
    - The violent behavior they observe in the media does not represent the behavior of most people.
    - The apparently aggressive behaviors they watch are not real.
    - Most people resolve conflicts by nonviolent means.
    - The real-life consequences of violence are harmful to the victim.

  -

Chapter 7: Memory: Remembrance of Things Past—and Future

Kinds of Memory

- Psychologists debate whether there are different systems of memory or just different examples of the same system.
  - Explicit memory.
    - referred to as declarative memory is memory for specific information.
    - Episodic Memory.
    - Semantic Memory.
- Implicit Memory: referred to as nondeclarative memory is memory of how to perform a task, how to do something.
- Retrospective Memory involves recalling information that has been previously learned. This includes:
  - Episodic
  - Semantic
  - Implicit
- Prospective memory involves remembering to do things in the future.
  - Prospective memory tends to fail when we are:
    - Preoccupied, distracted, feeling the stress of time pressure.
  - Various types of prospective memory tasks include:
    - Habitual tasks
    - Event based tasks
    - Time based tasks
- Retrospective and prospective memory decline with age.
- Moods and attitudes have an effect on prospective memory in that negative emotional states impair prospective memory.

Processes of Memory

- Encoding
  - Information about the outside world reaches our senses in the form of physical and chemical stimuli.
  - When we encode information we transform it into psychological formats that can be represented mentally.
    -

Processes of Memory

- Storage:
  - maintaining information over time.
- Retrieval:
  - Retrieval of stored information requires locating it and returning it to consciousness.

Stages of Memory:

- Atkinson-Shiffrin model of memory:
  - There are three stages of memory

- Sensory memory
- Short-term memory
- Long-term memory
- Information progresses through these stages determining how whether and how long the information will be retained.

Sensory Memory

- Sensory Memory is the type of memory that is first encountered by a stimulus.
    - Vision example:
        - Saccadic eye movements: series of eye fixations; movements which jump from one point to another about four times each second.
        - Memory trace: visual impression left by the stimulus.
        - Held in visual sensory register.
        - Research has used the whole report procedure and the partial report procedure in memory tasks.
    - Memory trace for visual stimuli decay within a second.
- Iconic Memory
    - Visual stimuli are referred to as icons. The sensory register that holds icons is labeled iconic memory.
    - Iconic memories are accurate, photographic memories but briefly stored.
- Iconic Memory and Saccadic Eye Movements.
    - Saccadic eye movements occur about four times every second.
    - Iconic memory holds icons for up to a second.
- Echoic Memory.
    - Mental representations of sounds, or auditory stimuli, are called echoes.
    - The sensory register that holds echoes is called echoic memory.
    - Echoic memory can last for several seconds.
    - By selectively attending to certain stimuli we sort them out from background noise.

Short-Term Memory

- If one focuses on a stimulus in the sensory register, they will tend to retain it in short-term memory (also referred to as working memory).
- In short term memory the image tends to significantly fade after 10-12 seconds if it is not rehearsed.
- To retain the information then rehearsal is needed.
    - The Serial-Position Effect.
    - Chunking.
    - Interference in Short-Term Memory.
- The Serial-Position Effect.
    - The tendency to recall the first and last items in a series is known as the serial-position effect.
- Chunking:
    - discrete elements of information.

- Interference in Short-Term Memory.
  - Prevention of rehearsal can inhibit short term memory.
  - Appearance of new information can displace the old information.

Long-Term Memory

- Long-term memory is the third stage of information processing.
- How Accurate Are Long-Term Memories?
  - Loftus notes that memories are distorted by our biases and needs.
  - We represent our world in the form of schemas.

CONTROVERSY IN PSYCHOLOGY: Can We Trust Eyewitness Testimony?

- The words chosen by an experimenter and those chosen by a lawyer interrogating a witness have been shown to influence the reconstruction of memories.
- Children tend to be more suggestible witnesses than adults.
  - When questioned properly, young children can provide accurate and useful testimony.
  - Hypnosis does more than amplify memories; it can also distort them
  - Witnesses may accept and embellish suggestions made by the hypnotist.
  - Witnesses may pay more attention to the suspect's clothing than to more meaningful characteristics such as facial features, height and weight.
- Other problems with eye-witness testimony are:
  - Identification is less accurate when suspects belong to ethnic groups that differ from that of the witness.
  - Identification of suspects is confused when interrogators make misleading suggestions.
  - Witnesses are seen as more credible when they claim to be certain in their testimony but there is little evidence that claims of certainty are accurate.

How Much Information Can Be Stored in Long-Term Memory?

- For all practical purposes, long-term memory is unlimited.
- Information can become lost but not destroyed or deleted.
- Transferring Information from Short-Term to Long-Term Memory:
  - The more often chunks of information are rehearsed, the more likely they are to be transferred to long-term memory.
  - Repeating information over and over to prevent it from decaying is termed maintenance rehearsal.
  - A more effective method is to make information more meaningful;
    - relating information to well-known material is termed elaborative rehearsal.
- Levels of Processing Information.

- Elaborative rehearsal involves processing information at a deeper level than maintenance rehearsal.
- Information is remembered if:
  - processed deeply-attended to,
  - encoded carefully, pondered, and
  - related to things we already know.
- Remembering relies on how deeply we processes information.
- Research has shown that deep processing is related to activity in the prefrontal area of the cerebral cortex.

- Flashbulb Memories:
  - The tendency to remember events that are surprising, important, and emotionally stirring.
  - Organizations in Long-Term Memory.

The Tip-of-the-Tongue-Phenomenon.

- The Tip-of-the-Tongue-Phenomenon.
  - The tip-of-the-tongue-phenomenon is the feeling of knowing an experience. Why?
    - Words were unfamiliar so elaborative rehearsal did not take place.
    - Seems to reflect incomplete learning.
    - Our knowledge of the topic may be incomplete, we don't know the specific answer but we know something.

Context-Dependent Memory

- The context in which we acquire information can also play a role in retrieval.
- Context-dependent memories are clear in the context in which they were formed.
- Context for memory extends to language.
- Déjà vu: the feeling that we know this person or have been there before.
  -

State-Dependent Memory

- State-dependent memory is an extension of context-dependent memory.
  - We retrieve information better when we are in the physiological or emotional state that is similar to the one in which we encoded and stored the information.
  - There is evidence of support for this with love, anger, frustration, rage, sober or inebriated, happy, sad, and bipolar.

Forgetting

- Ebbinghaus and the research with nonsense syllables.
  - Remembering should depend on simple acoustic coding and maintenance rehearsal rather than on elaborative rehearsal.
- Memory Tasks Used in Measuring Forgetting.
  - Recognition.
    - Failure to recognize something we have

experienced.
- Recall.
  - Remembering information from memory without cues.
- Relearning.
  - We can relearn information more rapidly the second time.

- Interference Theory.
  - We may forget information in short-term and long-term memory because newly learned material interferes with it.
    - Retroactive interference.
    - Proactive interference.

- Repression
  - Freud suggested that we are motivated to forget painful memories because they produce anxiety, guilt, and shame. (Repression)

CONTROVERSY IN PSYCHOLOGY:

- Do People Really Recover Repressed Memories of Sexual Abuse at an Early Age, Or Are These "Memories" Implanted by Interviewers?
  - Many recovered memories are sometime induced by therapists.
  - Techniques used to recover memories: hypnosis and guided imagery.

Infantile Amnesia

- Infantile amnesia is difficulty in remembering episodes that happened prior to age 3 or so.
- Has little to do with the fact that the episodes occurred in the distant past.
- Reflects the interaction of physiological and cognitive factors.

Anterograde and Retrograde Amnesia.

- Anterograde amnesia is memory lapses for the period following a trauma.
    - This memory loss has been linked to damage to the hippocampus.
- Retrograde amnesia is memory lapses for the period before the accident.

The Biology of Memory

- Engrams are viewed as electrical circuits in the brain the correspond to memory traces.
- Neural Activity and Memory:
  - The storage of experience appears to require the number of avenues of communication among brain cells to be increased.
  - Sea snails can be conditioned to they release more serotonin at certain synapses.
- Neural Activity and Memory:

- Acetylcholine (ACh) is vital in memory formation. Low levels of ACh are connected with Alzheimer's disease.
- Glutamate in the brain promotes conditioning.
- Adrenaline and noradrenaline both strengthen memory when they are released into the bloodstream following learning.
- Vasopressin facilitates memory (particularly working memory).
- Estrogen and testosterone facilitate working memory.

- Brain Structures and Memory.
  - Hippocampus is involved in the formation of new memories.
  - Parts of memories are stored in appropriate areas of the sensory cortex.
  - The limbic system is largely responsible for integrating these pieces of information when we recall an event.
  - The prefrontal cortex acts apparently as the executive center in memory.
  - Thalamus is involved in verbal memories.

LIFE CONNECTIONS:
Using the Psychology of Memory to Enhance Your Memory.

- Psychologists have developed methods for improving memory.
  - Drill and Practice: "A,B, C, D, ..."
  - Recommendations from Herrmann (1991) to remember a person's name:
    - Say the name out loud.
    - Ask the person a question, using her or his name.
    - Use the person's name as many times as you can during your conversation.
    - Write down the name when the conversation has ended.
  - Relate New Information to What Is Already Known.
    - Elaborative rehearsal.
- Form Unusual, Exaggerated Associations.
- Use the Method of Loci
- Use Mediation
- Use Mnemonic Devices

Chapter 8: Cognition and Language

Cognition

- Cognition (or thinking) may be defined as:
  - The mental activity involved in understanding, processing, and communicating information.
  - Cognition entails attending to information, representing it mentally, reasoning about it, and making judgments and decisions about it.
  - Conscious, planned attempts to make sense of our world.

Concepts

- Concepts are mental categories used to group together objects, relations, events, and abstractions.
  - Qualities that have common properties.

- Cognition involves:
  - categorizing new concepts and
  - manipulating relationships among concepts.

- We tend to organize concepts in hierarchies.

- Prototypes: examples that best match the essential features of categories.

- Overextension is overinclusion of instances in a category.

Problem Solving

- Approaches to Problem Solving
  - Flash of insight.
  - Finding rules.

- Understanding the Problem.
  - Focus on the right information.
  - Background knowledge helps.
  - Successful understanding of a problem requires three features:
    - The parts or elements of our mental representation of the problem relate to one another in a meaningful way.
    - The elements of our mental representations of the problem correspond to the elements of the problem in the outer world.
    - We have a storehouse of background knowledge that we can apply to the problem.

- Algorithms:
  - a specific procedure for solving a type of problem.
    - Algorithms invariable lead to the solution.
    - Systematic random search algorithm:
      - every possible combination is examined.

Problem Solving

- Heuristics: are rules of thumb that help us simplify and solve problems.
  - Heuristics do not guarantee a correct solution to a problem.

- Means-end analysis: assess the difference between our current situation and our goals and then do what we can to reduce this discrepancy.
- An analogy is a partial similarity among things that are different in other ways.
  - The analogy heuristic applies the solution of an earlier problem to the solution of a new one.

Factors That Affect Problem Solving
- Experts solve problems more efficiently and rapidly than novices do.
- Mental Sets:
  - the tendency to respond to a new problem with the same approach that helped solve similar problems.
- Insight:
  - Aha!: It seems as if pieces of information in the problem have suddenly been reorganized so that the solution leaps out at you.
- Incubation:
  - standing back from the problem may allow for insight.
- Functional Fixedness:
  - hinder problem solving by thinking of an object in terms of its name or its familiar function.

Heuristics in Decision Making
- Representative Heuristic:
  - people make judgments about events according to the populations of events that they appear to represent.
- Availability Heuristic:
  - our estimates of frequency or probability are based on how easy it is to find examples of relevant events.
- Anchoring and Adjustment Heuristics:
  - there can be a good deal of inertia in our judgments.
- The Framing Effect
  - wording, or the context in which information is presented, can influence decision making.

Overconfidence
- Overconfidence applies to judgments.
  - Many people refuse to alter their judgments even in the face of statistical evidence that shows them to be flawed.
- 20-20 hindsight: "we knew it all along".
- There are several reasons for overconfidence:
  - We tend to be unaware of how flimsy our assumptions may be.
  - We tend to focus on examples that confirm our judgments and ignore those that do not.
  - We tend to forget information that is counter to our judgments.
  - We work to bring about the events we believe in, so they sometimes become self-fulfilling prophecies.
  - Even when people are told that they tend to be overconfident in their decisions, they usually ignore

this information.

Language

- Language is the communication of thoughts and feelings by means of symbols that are arranged to rules of grammar.
  - In recent years our exclusive claim to language has also been questioned.
  - Language is one of the human assets that has enabled us to survive and prosper.
  - True language is distinguished from the communication systems of lower animals by properties such as semanticity, infinite creativity, and displacement.
    - Semanticity.
    - Infinite creativity.
    - Displacement.
- Language and Cognition.
  - Can a person think without using language?
  - Jean Piaget believed that language reflects knowledge of the world but that much knowledge can be acquired without language.
- The Linguistic-Relativity Hypothesis.
  - The linguistic-relativity hypothesis: language structures the way we perceive the world.
  - Infants display considerable intelligence before they have learned to speak.

Language Development: Two Year Explosion

- Prelinguistic vocalizations include crying, cooing, and babbling.
- Children tend to utter their first word at about 1 year of age.
- Development of Grammar.
  - Holophrases: single words that can express complex meanings.
  - Toward the end of the second year children begin to speak two-word sentences termed telegraphic speech.
- Overregularization.
  - Grammatical rules for forming the past tense and plurals.
  - The tendency to regularize the irregular.
  - Reflects knowledge of grammar not faulty language development.
  - By the age of 6, children's vocabularies have expanded to 10,000 words.
  - By 7 to 9, most children realize that words can have more than one meaning.

Nature and Nurture in Language Development

- Genetic and Environmental Factors In Language Development.
  - Nativist theory of language hold that language development is innate or inborn.

- Psycholinguistic theory: language acquisition involves the interaction of environmental influences such as:
  - exposure to parental speech,
  - Reinforcement, and
  - an inborn tendency to acquire language.
- Language acquisition device (LAD) prepares the nervous system to learn grammar.
  - Universal grammar:
    - an underlying set of rules for turning ideas into sentences.
- Genetic and Environmental Factors In Language Development.
  - Language development reflects the interactions between the influences of heredity (nature) and the environment (nurture).
  - Learning theorists see language developing according to imitation and reinforcement.
    - Parents serve as models.
    - Learning theory cannot account for:
      - the unchanging sequence of language development,
      - and the spurts in children's language acquisition.

LIFE CONNECTION: Bilingualism and Ebonics – Making Connections or Building Walls?

- Most people throughout the world speak two or more languages.
  - For more than 30 million people in the U.S. English is a second language.
  - Bilingualism and Intellectual Development.
    - Most linguists consider it advantageous for children to be bilingual.
- Williams, a psychologist, developed a test that was culturally sensitive to African American children called the Black Intelligence Test of Cultural Homogeneity .
- Ebonics derives from the word ebony and phonics.
    - There are differences between Ebonics and standard English in the use of verbs.
    - In this case many African Americans are in effect bilingual.

Chapter 9: Intelligence and Creativity

Intelligence

- Definitions of intelligence include:
  - Intelligence permits us to adapt to conditions and to challenge our physical limitations.
  - Intelligence is broadly thought of as the underlying ability to understand the world and cope with its challenges.

- Intelligence allows people to:
  - Think.
  - Understand complex ideas.
  - Reason.
  - Solve problems.
  - Learn from experience.
  - Adapt to the environment.

Theories of Intelligence

- Factor theories argue that intelligence is made up of a number of mental abilities ranging from one to hundreds.

- Charles Spearman suggested that intelligence has an underlying factor called "g" for general intelligence. "g" is broad reasoning and problem solving skills.

- Louis Thurstone used factor analysis and suggested eight specific factors which he labeled primary mental abilities.
  - Visual and spatial abilities.
  - Perceptual speed.
  - Numerical ability.
  - Verbal meaning.
  - Memory.
  - Word Fluency.
  - Deductive reasoning.
  - Inductive reasoning.

- Theory of Multiple Intelligences
  - Howard Gardner proposed that intelligence is comprised of different kinds of intelligences.
  - He proposed that each intelligence has its neurological base in a different area of the brain.

- The Triarchic Theory of Intelligence.
  - Robert Sternberg proposed an intelligence with three types: analytical, creative, and practical.

CONTROVERSY IN PSYCHOLOGY:
Is "Emotional Intelligence" a form of intelligence?

- Social and emotional skills are a form of intelligence.
  - These are similar to Gardner's proposed intrapersonal and interpersonal skills.
  - Should these be taught in schools?
  - Critics state that these areas are important for determining life outcomes but there is nothing to gain by calling them intelligences.

Creativity and Intelligence.

- Creativity may be defined as the ability to do things that are novel and useful.

- Creative people share characteristics that include:
  - They take chances.
  - They refuse to accept limitations.
  - They appreciate art and music.
  - They use materials around them to make unique things.
  - They challenge social norms.
  - They take unpopular stands.
  - They examine ideas that other people accept at face value.

- Two types of thinking:
  - Convergent thinking:
  - Divergent thinking:
  - Problem solving can involve both kinds of thinking.

- Research indicates that relationships between intelligence test scores and standard measures of creativity is only moderate.

The Measurement of Intelligence

- The Stanford-Binet Intelligence Scale.
  - In 1905 the Binet-Simon scale was created.
  - The Binet-Simon scale yielded a score called a mental age (MA). The MA indicates the intellectual level at which the child is functioning.
  - Louis Terman, working at Stanford University, adapted the test for use with children in the U.S. The test came to be known as the Stanford-Binet Intelligence Scale (SBIS).

- The Stanford-Binet Intelligence Scale continued.
  - The SBIS yielded an intelligence quotient (IQ) rather than a mental age. IQ reflects the relationship between a child's mental age and their actual chronological age.
  - IQ = mental age (MA) / chronological age (CA) X 100.

Weschler Scales

- Wechsler developed a series of scales where each subtest measures a different intellectual task.
  - These scales can be grouped into:
    - Verbal tasks: require knowledge of verbal concepts.
    - Performance tasks: require familiarity with spatial-relations concepts.

- Wechsler introduced the concept of the deviation IQ. He based IQ on how a person's answers compared with those attained by people in the same age group. The average level is defined as an IQ score of 100.

- Group Tests.
  - first developed during World War I for use with large numbers of people in schools and the armed forces.

Socioeconomic and Ethnic Differences in Intelligence.

- Lower-class U.S. children obtain IQ scores 10 to 15 points lower than those obtained by middle and upper class children.

- African American children tend to obtain IQ scores 15 points lower than those obtained by European American age-mates.
  - Most psychologists believe that ethnic differences such as these reflect cultural attitudes toward education rather than inborn racial differences.
  - Steinberg claims that parental encouragement, supervision, and peer support for academic achievement partially explain the superior performance of European Americans and Asian Americans.

Extremes of Intelligences

- Mental Retardation.
  - Mental retardation refers to substantial limitations in present functioning characterized by significantly sub-average intellectual functioning existing concurrently with related limitations in two or more of the following applicable adaptive skill areas:
    - Communication.
    - Self care.
    - Home living.
    - Social skills.
    - Community use.
    - Self direction.
    - Health and safety.
    - Functional academics.
    - Leisure and work.
  - Most children who are retarded are mildly retarded. They are likely to be taught in regular classrooms and are capable of adjusting to the demands of society at large.
  - Causes of mental retardation include:
    - Chromosomal abnormalities such as Down syndrome.
    - Genetic disorders such as phenylketonuria.
    - Brain damage.

- Giftedness.
  - Children who have outstanding abilities, are capable of high performance in a specific academic area such as language arts or mathematics, or who show creativity or leadership, or have talent in physical activities.
  - Terman's study of geniuses:
    - Studied children with IQ scores above 135; average score was 150.
    - As a group they were extremely successful in terms of level of education, socioeconomic status, and creativity.
    - They were well adjusted with rates of psychological disorders and suicide below the

national average.

The Testing Controversy

- A survey of psychologists in 1987 found that most consider intelligence tests to be culturally biased against African Americans and member so the lower classes.

- Intelligence tests measure traits that are required in developed, high-tech societies.

- The tests seem to reflect middle-class European American culture.

Culture-Free Intelligence Tests?

- Psychologists are trying to construct "culture-free" tests.
    - Cattell: Culture-Fair Intelligence Test
    - Goodenough's Draw-A-Person test

- Culture-free tests have not lived up to promise.

- Intelligence tests measure traits required in developed, high-tech societies.

- Broad achievements in tests reflect intelligence but also reflect familiarity with cultural concepts required to answer test questions correctly.

Nature and Nurture in Intelligence.

- The Bell Curve Hernstein and Murray asserts
    - IQ is an accurate measure of intelligence
    - Intelligence is mainly due to heredity.
    - Overall intelligence in US is declining, because people with less intelligence are having more children.
    - US is becoming divided into larger lower class of people with low intelligence and smaller class of wealthier people higher intelligence.

- Critics charge that IQ is affected by early learning experiences, academic and vocational motivation , and formal education.

Genetic Influences on Intelligence.

- Research includes kinship studies, twin studies and adoptee studies.

- IQ scores of identical twins are more alike than scores for any other pairs.

- All in all, studies generally suggest that the heritability of intelligence is between 40% and 60%.

Determinants of Intelligence

- Environmental Influences on Intelligence.
    - Research methods include:
        - manipulation of the testing situation,
        - observation of the role of the home environment, and
        - the evaluation of the effects of educational programs.
    - Stereotype Vulnerability
    - The Home Environment and Style of Parenting.

CONTROVERSY IN PSYCHOLOGY: The Mozart Effect

- Listening to and studying music may enhance spatial reasoning.
  - Claims that listening to 10 minutes of Mozart's Piano Sonata K 448 enhanced college students' scores on spatial reasoning tasks.
  - Musical training develops the neural firing patterns used in spatial reasoning.

Other Factors Related to Intelligence

- Education.
  - Education contributes to intelligence.
- Adoptee Studies.
  - Intellectual functioning would appear to reflect the interaction of genetic physical, personal and sociocultural.

Evaluation of The Bell Curve

- Intellectual functioning appears to reflect a complex web of
  - Genetic,
  - Physical,
  - Personal,
  - And sociocultural factors.
- Evidence clearly argues for a more balanced view than that of The Bell Curve.

Life Connections: Enhancing Intellectual Functioning

- Intellectual functioning changes with age, experiences, education and many other factors.
- Many things you can do to enhance your child's intellectual functioning
  - Provide safe home.
  - Be emotionally and verbally responsive
  - Provide a variety of experiences.
  - Encourage your children to be independent.
  - Make sure your children know the educational basics.
  - Consider giving your children training in music.
- Factors that contribute to adults' intellectual functioning
  - General Health.
  - Socioeconomic status.
  - Stimulating activities.
  - Marriage to a spouse with a high level of intellectual functioning.
  - Openness to new experience.

Chapter 10: Motivation and Emotion

The Psychology of Motivation

- The psychology of motivation concerns the whys of behavior.

- Motives are hypothetical states that activate behavior towards goals. Motives may take the form of:
  - Needs
    - Physiological
    - Psychological
  - Drives
  - Incentives

Theories of Motivation

- Psychologists do not agree about the precise nature of motivation.

- The Evolutionary Perspective
  - Animals naturally prewired to respond to certain stimuli in certain ways.
  - Species-specific behaviors are called instincts or fixed action patterns.

- Drive Reductionism and Homeostasis
  - Primary drives trigger arousal (tension) and activate behavior. We engage in behaviors that reduce the tension.
  - Acquired drives are acquired through experience.
  - Homeostasis is a steady state. People are motivated to maintain a steady state.

- The Search for Stimulation
  - Stimulus motives: the organism is motivated to increase stimulation not reduce a drive.
    - Lower animals and humans appear to be motivated to seek novel stimulation.
    - Stimulus motivation provides an evolutionary advantage. Animals that are active and motivated to learn about their environment are more likely to survive.

- Humanistic Theory
  - Abraham Maslow believed that people are motivated by the conscious desire for personal growth.
    - Self-actualization:
      - self initiated striving to become whatever we believe we are capable of being.
    - Maslow's hierarchy of needs ranges from physiological needs such as hunger and thirst through self actualization.
  - Critics argue that there is too much individual variation for the hierarchy of motives to apply to everyone.

Hunger

- Importance of food.
  - Necessary for survival.

- Symbol of family togetherness and caring.
- We associate food with the nurturance of the parent-child relationship.
- Biological Influences on Hunger.
  - Satiety or satisfaction.
  - Hunger pangs are stomach contractions.
  - Ventromedial nucleus of the hypothalamus.
    - The stop eating center of the brain.
  - Lateral hypothalamus
  - is the start eating center of the brain.
- Psychological Influences of Hunger.
  - Other factors that influence hunger include:
    - Aroma of food,
    - Anxiety or depression, or
    - Boredom.

Anorexia Nervosa

- A life threatening eating disorder characterized by:
  - Extreme fear of being too heavy.
  - Dramatic weight loss.
  - Distorted body image.
  - Resistance to eating enough to maintain a healthy weight.
- Afflicts:
  - Women during adolescence and young adulthood.
  - European American females of higher socioeconomic status.
  - Increase in numbers in recent years.
- Risks:
  - Mortality rate is approximately 5%.
  - Osteoporosis.

Bulimia Nervosa

- Characterized by recurrent cycles of binging and purging.
  - Purging can include:
    - vomiting,
    - strict dieting,
    - fasting,
    - laxatives, and
    - prolonged exercise.

Origins of Eating Disorders

- Psychodynamic theory:
  - coping with sexual fear, regressing to life prior to puberty.
  - The family environment is negative.
    - Typically a history of child abuse.
  - Exposure to high parental expectations.
- Sociocultural perspective.
  - Slimness is idealized.
- Genetic perspective
  - Tends to run in families.

- Genetic factors might not directly cause eating disorders but are likely to involve obsessionistic and perfectionistic personality traits.

Aggression

- Explanations for Aggression:
  - Social deprivation and inequality.
  - Act aggressively to establish and defend land (territory).
- Biology, Chemistry, and Aggression.
  - Instinctive aggressive reactions in lower animals may be automatic.
  - Chemistry:
    - Testosterone appears to affect the tendencies to dominate and control other people.

Aggression

- Psychological Aspects of Aggression.
  - Psychodynamic Theory and Aggression.
    - Freud believed that aggression is natural and instinctive.
    - Steam engine analogy; by holding in steam rather than venting it we set the stage for future explosions.
  - Cognitive Psychology and Aggression.
    - Behavior is influenced by our values, by how we interpret situations, and by choice.
    - Aggression is not automatic: people decide.

CONTROVERSY IN PSYCHOLOGY: The Catharsis Controversy.

- Venting of aggressive impulses is termed catharsis.
  - This is a safety valve.
  - Possibly leading to pleasant reductions in tension,
  - Some research indicates that it may encourage more aggression later.

Cross Cultural Aspects of Aggression
Cultural Characteristics.
  - Stereotype of aggressive male is not universal.
    - Likely that people arrive at consensus as to what proper behavior is and teach their children accordingly.
- Psychological Aspects of Aggression continued.
  - Learning and Aggression.
    - Learning is acquired through reinforcement thus reinforced aggression is more likely to be repeated.
    - Aggressive skills are mainly acquired by the observation of other people.

Situational factors can contribute to aggression.
  - In mobs people may experience deindividuation which is a state of reduced self awareness. This includes:

- anonymity,
- sharing of responsibility (diffusion of responsibility),
- high level of emotional arousal, and
- a focus on the group's norms.
  – Environmental factors leading to aggressive behavior include:
    - Bad smelling pollutants.
    - Extreme noise.
    - Extreme heat.

Achievement Motivation
Assessment of Motivation.
  – Thematic Apperception Test (TAT).
    - TAT contains cards with pictures and drawings that are subject to various interpretations.
  – People with high motivation:
    - Earn higher grades.
    - Likely to earn higher salaries and be promoted.
    - Better at math.
  – Different Forces that drive motivation:
    - Tangible rewards.
    - Performance goals are usually met through extrinsic rewards.
    - Learning goals usually lead to intrinsic rewards.

Emotion

- Emotions are feeling states with physiological, cognitive, and behavioral components.
  – Arousal of the autonomic nervous system.
    - Sympathetic nervous system: rapid heartbeat, breathing, sweating, muscle tension.
  – Behavioral tendencies occur with emotions.
    - For example fear leads to avoidance or escape and anger may lead to "pay back" behaviors.
  – Parasympathetic nervous system arousal can also occur.
    - Joy, grief, jealousy, disgust, etc. all have cognitive, physiological, and behavioral components.

The Expression of Emotions

- Expression of many emotions may be universal.

- However, not perfect one-to-one relationship between facial expressions and emotions.

Positive Psychology.
Deals with positive emotions such as happiness and love.

- Statistics of those who are happy.
  – Majority of people in developed nations are satisfied with their lives.

- Happiness tends to run in families.
- People tend to be happier when they live in affluent societies and earn decent incomes.
- Money does not make people happy but when we have enough money at least we don't have to worry about money.
- More educated people tend to be happier.

- Statistics of those who are happy continued.
  - People who are married are happier.
  - People who have a social support are happier.
  - Happy people are more open to new experiences and are more willing to risk.
  - Religious people are happier.
  - Happiness tends to be accompanied by optimism.

- Suggestions to be happy include:
  - Take advantage of your education to develop skills so that you can be free from want.
  - Do not let the fact that others have more impair your ability to appreciate what you have.
  - Value friendships and other social relationships.
  - Think about the meaning of life and make your life more meaningful.
  - Consider whether you blame yourself too much when things go wrong.
  - Consider if you are generally optimistic or pessimistic about your future.

Theories of Emotions

- James-Lange Theory.
  - Emotions follow rather than cause behavioral response to events.
  - We become angry because we are acting aggressively.
  - We may be able to change our feelings by changing our behavior.

- Cannon-Bard Theory.
  - Events might simultaneously trigger bodily responses and the experience of emotion.
  - Emotions accompany bodily responses.

- Theory of Cognitive Appraisal (Schachter and Singer)
  - The label we give to an emotion depends on cognitive appraisal of the situation.

A CLOSER LOOK: Just What Do Lie Detectors Detect?

- Body Reactions to Lying:
  - Facial expressions often offer clues to deceit.
  - Sympathetic arousal symptoms include dry mouth

- Lie detector tests (Polygraphs) monitor sympathetic arousal.
  - Indicators include:
  - heart rate.
    - Blood pressure.
    - Respiration rate.
    - Electrodermal response (sweating).
  - American Polygraph Association claims that

polygraphs are 85-95% accurate.
- Research on psychologists' opinion of accuracy indicate that most think it is not theoretically sound and should not be used in a court of law.

LIFE CONNECTIONS: Obesity

- Facts about obesity:
- Origins of Obesity.
    - Biological side points to the influence of heredity.
        - Obesity runs in families.
        - Set point: the point at which the hunger drive kicks in because of fat deficiency in cells.
        - Fatty tissue also metabolizes food more slowly than muscle does.
        - Dieting slows down the metabolic rate thus making it more difficult to lose weight.

Weight Control

- Shedding excess pounds lowers the risk of health problems such as diabetes and heart disease.
- The most effective weight control programs involve:
    - Improving nutritional knowledge.
    - Decreasing caloric intake.
    - Exercising.
    - Changing eating habits.
    - Eating more fresh fruits and vegetables.
    - Cutting down on butter, margarine, oils, and sugar.
- Strategies for weight loss include:
    - Establishing calorie intake goals.
    - Substitute low calorie foods.
    - Take a 5-minute break between helpings.
    - Avoid temptations.
    - Exercise
    - Reward yourself but not with food.
    - Use imagery.
    - Mentally walk through various scenarios.
    - Above all if you slip, don't blow it out of proportion.

Chapter 11: Personality: Theory and Measurement

Introduction to Personality

- Psychologists define personality as the reasonably stable patterns of emotions, motives, and behavior that distinguish one person from another.

Theories of Personality: Psychodynamic Perspective

- Sigmund Freud characterized personality as conflict, a dynamic struggle.
  - Drives like sex, aggression and the need for superiority conflict with laws, social rules and moral codes.
  - At some time the laws are internalized.
  - The conflict is between opposing inner forces.

- Psychosexual Development.
  - The human mind is like an iceberg.

- Psychosexual Development.
  - Repression is the automatic ejection of anxiety-evoking ideas from awareness.
  - To explore the unconscious mind, Freud engaged in a form of mental detective work called psychoanalysis.
    - Talk about anything that pops into their mind.
    - Resistance:
      - the desire to avoid thinking about or discussing thoughts.

- The Structure of Personality.
  - Psychic structures or mental structures that are the clashing forces of personality. Freud proposed that there are three psychic structures:
    - Id
    - Ego
    - Superego

Psychodynamic Perspective: The Structure of Personality

- The Id
  - The id is present at birth and represents physiological drives and is entirely unconscious.

- The ego
  - stands for reason and good sense, for rational ways of coping with frustration.

- The Superego
  - develops throughout childhood, usually incorporating the moral standards and values of parents through identification.

- Eros: is aimed at preserving and perpetuating life.

- Libido: psychic energy involving sexual impulses.
  - Focused on sexual feelings in different parts of the body or erogenous zones.

- Five periods of psychosexual development:
  - Oral
  - Anal
  - Phallic
  - Latency
  - Genital
- Oral stage:
  - during the first year of life. If it fits into the mouth then it goes in the mouth (e.g. sucking and biting).
- Anal stage:
  - gratification is attained through contraction and relaxation of the muscles that control elimination of waste products from the body.
- Latency stage:
  - sexual feelings remain unconscious.
- Genital stage:
  - final stage, find sexual gratification through intercourse with a member of the other gender.

Theories of Personality: Other Psychodynamic Theorists

- Carl Jung, a Swiss psychiatrist developed his own psychodynamic theory called analytical psychology.
  - Jung downplayed the importance of the sexual instinct.
  - Collective unconscious:
    - contains primitive images called archetypes that reflect the history of our species.
- Alfred Adler .
  - Inferiority complex: people are motivated by this complex.
  - Creative self:
    - a self aware aspect of personality that strives to overcome obstacles and develop the individual's potential.
  - Adler's view has been termed individual psychology.
- Karen Horney.
  - Horney argued that in contrast to Freud's view, little girls do not feel inferior to boys.
  - the view that girls are inferior is founded on Western cultural prejudice, not scientific evidence.
  - Unconscious sexual and aggressive impulses are less important than social relationships in children's development.
  - Genuineness and consistent love can alleviate the effects of even the most traumatic childhood.
- Erik Erikson.
  - Social relationships are more crucial than sexual urges.
  - We are the conscious architects of our own personalities.
  - Proposed stages of psychosocial development.

Theories of Personality:
Evaluation of the Psychodynamic Perspective

- Psychodynamic theory focused attention on the far-reaching effects of childhood events.

- Important for parents to be aware of emotional needs of children.

- Defense mechanisms have become part of everyday speech.

- Psychic structures may be too vague to measure scientifically.

- Oedipus and Electra complexes remain little more than speculation.

The Trait Perspective

- Traits are reasonably stable elements of personality that are inferred from behavior.

- From Hippocrates to the Present.
  - Hippocrates believed that traits are embedded in four basic bodily fluids (humors).
  - Gordon Allport catalogued approximately 18,000 human traits from dictionaries.

- Hans Eysenck's Trait Theory.
  - Eysenck focused his research on two personality traits:
    - Introversion-extraversion
    - Emotional stability-instability (neuroticism).

- The Five-Factor Model (The Big Five).
  - Recent research has focused on five basic personality factors:
    - Extraversion
    - Conscientiousness
    - Agreeableness
    - Openness
    - Neuroticism
  - The factors are related to basic temperaments and are largely inborn.
  - McCrae and Costa created the NEO Five Factor Inventory which has been used in numerous research projects.

- Evaluation of the Trait Perspective.
  - Trait theorists have focused much attention on the development of personality tests.
  - Trait theory has tended to be more descriptive than explanatory.
  - Sometimes criticized as being circular.

Learning-Theory Perspectives

- Behaviorism views that personality is plastic-that situational variables and environmental influences are the key shapers of human preference and behaviors.

- Social-Cognitive Theory is a contemporary view of

learning developed by Bandura. Focuses on the importance of learning by observation.

- Social-Cognitive Theory
  - Observational Learning (modeling).
    - Acquiring knowledge by observing others.
    - Our expectations stem from our observations of what happens to ourselves and other people.

Person Variables

- Competencies
  - include knowledge of rules that guide conduct, concepts about ourselves and other people, and skills.

- Encoding Strategies
  - Some people make themselves miserable by encoding events in self-defeating ways.

- Expectancies:
  - Self efficacy
    - Beliefs that we can accomplish certain things.
  - Expectancies involve what will happen if we engage in certain behaviors.

- Emotions:
  - Because of different learning histories, similar situations can arouse different feelings in us.
  - Stimuli arouse feelings in us, and feelings influence our behavior

- Self-Regulatory Systems and Plans
  - Self-regulation helps us influence our environments. We can select the situations to which we expose ourselves.
  - We can to some degree select our responses within an environment.

Evaluation of the Learning Perspective

- Emphasized the importance of publicly observable variables or behaviors, if psychology is to be a science.

- Learning theorists emphasized the importance of environmental conditions as determinants of behavior.

- Behaviorism is limited in its ability to explain personality.
  - Behaviorism does not describe, explain or even suggest the richness of inner human experience.
  - Behaviorism may not pay enough attention to genetic variation.

The Humanistic-Existential Perspective

- Humanists and existentialists dwell on the meaning of life.
  - Self awareness is the hub of this search for meaning.

- Humanism puts people and self-awareness at the center of consideration. People are capable of:
  - Free choice.
  - Self fulfillment.
  - Ethical behavior.

- Existentialism:
  - giving personal meaning to things and making

personal choices.

- Maslow argued that people also have a conscious need for self-actualization-to become all that they can be.
- Carl Roger's Self Theory.
  - Rogers wrote people shape themselves through free choice and action.
  - Rogers defined the self as the center of experience.
  - Choices are made on the basis of your values.
  - The Self-Concept and Frames of Reference.
    - Self-concepts.
    - Frames of Reference.
- Self-esteem and Positive Regard.
  - Unconditional positive regard: accept people as having intrinsic merit regardless of their behavior at the moment.
  - The path to self-actualization requires getting in touch with our genuine feelings, accepting them, and acting upon them.
  - Rogers believed that we have
    - Self-ideals: mental images of what we are capable of becoming.
    - We are motivated to reduce the discrepancy between our self-concepts and our self-ideals.

Evaluation of the Humanistic-Existential Perspective

- Humanistic-Existential perspective helped emphasize the importance of personal experience.
- Humanistic-existential perspective see humans as free to make choices, assuming personal freedom.
- Conscious experience is private and subjective.
- Self-actualization yields circular explanations for behavior.
- Humanistic-existential perspective has little to say about the development of traits and personality types.

The Sociocultural Perspective

- Some psychologists believe that personality cannot be understood without reference to the sociocultural perspective.
- Individualism Versus Collectivism.
  - Individualists:
    - tend to define themselves in terms of their personal identities and to give priority to their personal goals.
  - Collectivists:
    - tend to define themselves in terms of the groups to which they belong and to give priority to the group's goals.
- Evaluation of the Sociocultural Perspective.
  - The sociocultural perspective provides valuable insights into the roles of ethnicity, gender, culture, and socioeconomic status in personality formation.
  - Sociocultural factors are external forces that are

internalized.
- The sociocultural perspective enhances our sensitivity to cultural differences.

Acculturation, Adjustment, and Self-Esteem: Just How Much Acculturation Is Enough?

- Acculturation:
  - activities in which immigrants become acclimated to the customs and behavior patterns of their new host culture.
- Self-esteem has been shown to be connected with patterns of acculturation among immigrants.
- People who identify with the bicultural pattern have the highest self-esteem.

Measurement of Personality

- Personality Assessment:
  - take a sample of behavior to predict future behavior.
    - Behavior-rating scales: trained observers check off each occurrence of a specific behavior within a certain time frame.
    - Aptitude assessment aids in gaining insight into whether individuals are suited for certain occupations.
- Objective Tests.
  - Objective tests present respondents with a standardized group of test items in the form of a questionnaire.
- The Minnesota Multiphasic Personality Inventory (MMPI) contains hundreds of items in a true-false format.
  - Used to diagnose psychological disorders.
  - Most widely used test in clinical work.
  - Most widely used personality measurement in psychological research.
  - MMPI scales were empirically constructed; based on actual clinical data rather than on psychological theory.
  - Confidence in the MMPI has developed because of its extensive use.

Projective Tests
- People are shown ambiguous stimuli such as inkblots or ambiguous drawings and asked to say what they look like.
  - People project their own personalities into their responses.
- The Rorschach Inkblot Test.
  - Individuals are shown inkblots and asked what they look like.
    - A response that reflects the shape of the blot is considered a sign of adequate reality testing.
    - A response that integrates several features of the blot is considered a sign of high intellectual functioning.

- Critics argue that there is little evidence to support the test's validity.
- The Thematic Apperception Test (TAT)
  - The test consists of drawings and subjects make up stories about them.
  - Widely used in research on motivation.

Life Connections: Understanding and Enhancing Self-Esteem.

- Our self-esteem is the value or worth that we attach to ourselves.

- Positive self-esteem is one of the keys to psychological adjustment.

Developmental Factors and Self-Esteem

- Learning Theory: self-esteem reflects ability to obtain reinforcements.

- Social Cognitive Theory: self-efficacy is based on success

- Roger's Self Theory: our self-esteem reflects the esteem of others

- Five-factor Model: certain personality traits will correlate positively with self-esteem.

Enhancing Self-Esteem.

- Change things you can and accept those things you can't change.

  - Improve Yourself.

  - Challenge the Realism of Your Ideal Self.

  - Stop Comparing Yourself to Others.

  - Substitute Realistic Goals for Unattainable Goals.

  - Build Self-Efficacy Expectations.

Chapter 12: Gender and Sexuality

Gender Stereotypes and Differences

- A gender stereotype is a fixed, conventional idea about how men and women ought to behave.

- Gender roles are clusters of gender stereotypes that reflect cultural beliefs.

- According to Lipsitz Bem, 3 beliefs have run through western thought.
    - Women and men have basically different psychological and sexual natures.
    - Men are the superior, dominant sex.
    - Gender differences and male superiority are "natural".

Gender Differences in Cognitive Skills

- Intelligence Assessments don't show overall gender differences in cognitive abilities.

- However, research does suggest some differences.
    - Females somewhat superior in verbal abilities. Girls seem to acquire language faster than boys.
    - Males somewhat superior in ability to manipulate images and visual-spatial abilities and in math.
    - In general, differences are small.

- Some differences may reflect cultural influences rather than inborn.

Gender Differences in Personality

- Feingold (1994,1998) findings:
    - Women are perceived to exceed men in sociability, happiness, anxiety, trust and nurturance.
    - Men are perceived to exceed women in social dominance and tough-mindedness.

Gender Differences in Social Behavior

- Key differences seem to exist regarding sex and aggression.
    - Men show more interest in sex than women; men report being more interested in casual sex and in multiple sex partners.
    - Generally, research shows that males behave more aggressively than females.

Gender Differences in Mate Selection

- Women tend to focus on professional status, consideration, dependability, kindness and fondness for children.

- Men tend to focus on physical allure, cooking ability and thrift.

Gender Typing-On Becoming A Woman or a Man.
The Roles of Evolution and Heredity.

- Buss (2000) suggests that gender differences were fashioned by natural selection.
- Evolutionary forces favor survival of women who desire status in their mates and men who favor physical allure because these preferences provide reproductive advantages.
  - This theory is largely speculative.
- Gender differences in the functioning and organization of the brain do exist.
  - Men use the hippocampus in both hemispheres when they are trying to navigate whereas women use only the hippocampus in the right hemisphere.
  - Men with damage to the left hemisphere are more likely to experience difficulties in verbal functioning than women with similar damage.
  - Men with damage to the right hemisphere are more likely to have problems with spatial relations than women with similar injuries.

The Role of Sex Hormones.
  - Substances that may masculinize or feminize the brain. These include: androgens and testosterone.
  - However, psychologists argue that boys and girls can choose whether or not to act aggressively regardless of hormone levels.

- Psychodynamic Theory and Gender-Typing.
  - Freud explained the acquisition of gender roles in terms of identification.
  - Research has shown that boys and girls are inclined to develop gender-typed preferences for toys and activities earlier than predicted by psychodynamic theory.

- Learning Theories and Gender-Typing.
  - Experience helps the individual create concepts of gender-appropriate behavior.
  - Children can learn what is masculine and feminine by observational learning.
  - Children are reinforced to imitate adults of the same gender.

- Gender-Schema Theory and Gender-Typing.
  - Gender-schema theory proposes that people look at the world through the lenses of gender.
    - Cultures tend to polarize females and males by organizing social life around mutually exclusive gender roles.
    - Research suggests that polarized female-male scripts serve as cognitive anchors within Western culture.

Sexual Motivation

- Hormones and Sexual Motivation
  - Testosterone replacement therapy increases sex drive.
  - Sex drive in women is also connected with testosterone levels.
  - Sex hormones have activating effects:

- they affect the sex drive, and
- promote sexual response.
  - Sex hormones also have organizing effects:
    - they motivate lower animals toward masculine or feminine mating patterns.

CONTROVERSY IN PSYCHOLOGY:
Is the human sex drive affected by pheromones?

- Pheromones are odorless chemicals that are detected through a "sixth sense" the vomeronasal organ (VNO).
  - There is a debate about whether or not the VNO works.
  - Not conclusive that pheromones directly affect the behavior of people.
  - Steroids suspected of being pheromones
  - The substances do not release sexual fixed action patterns (instincts).

Sexual Orientation

- Heterosexual orientation:
  - sexual attraction to people of the other sex.

- Homosexual orientation:
  - attracted to and interested in forming romantic relationships with people of their own sex.
    - Males are referred to as gay males.
    - Females are referred to as lesbians.
    - Bisexual people are attracted to both females and males.

- Sexual orientation differs from sexual activity.

Sexual Orientation

- Freudian theory
  - attributes sexual orientation to identification with male or female figures.

- Learning theory
  - look for roles of factors such as reinforcement and observational learning.

- Genetic factors.
  - 22% of the brothers of gay men were gay or bisexual.
  - 52% of identical twins were both gay.

- Sexual orientation has not been reliably linked with adolescent or adult levels of sex hormones.

- Much about the development of sexual orientation remains speculative.

Interpersonal Attraction

- Many aspects of beauty appear to be cross-cultural.
  - In one study, men found attractive the following qualities:
    - Large eyes.
    - High cheekbones.

75

- Narrow jaws.
  - In a study on what women find attractive the researchers discovered that tallness was an asset.
  - Preferences for body weight and shape may be more culturally determined.
  - "Pretty Is as Pretty Does?"
    - Both men and women are perceived as more attractive when they are smiling.
    - Women tend to prefer men who are outgoing, self-assertive, and self-confident.
    - Men tend to respond negatively to women who show self-assertion and social dominance.

The Matching Hypothesis

- People tend to date people who are similar to themselves in physical attractiveness.
  - One motive for this seems to be fear of rejection by more attractive people.

- Research findings show that:
  - Nearly 94% of single European American men have European American women as partners.
  - About 82% of African American men have African American women as partners.
  - About 83% of the women and men in the study chose partners within five years of their own age and of the same or a similar religion.

Interpersonal Attraction: Reciprocity

- Reciprocity is a powerful determinant of attraction.
  - We tend to return feelings of admiration.
  - We tend to be more open, warm and helpful when we are interacting with strangers who seem to like us.

Love

- Triangular model of love proposed by Sternberg includes three components: intimacy, passion, and commitment.

- The ideal form of love combines all three and is called consummate love.

- Romantic love is characterized by passion and intimacy.

- Men are generally more reluctant than women to make commitments in their romantic relationships.
  - The affective shift hypothesis suggests that
    - Women tend to experience a greater feeling of love and commitment-a positive affective shift-after first time sex than men do.
    - As a group, men are more likely than women to be interested in short-term relationships and multiple sex partners.
    - Men with high numbers of sex partners tend to experience a negative affective shift following first-time sex. This motives them to end the relationship.
    - Men with fewer sex partners and more of an interest in developing long-term relationships also tend to experience the positive affective shift after

first-time sex.

Sexual Response Cycle

- The changes that occur in the body of men and women when they become sexually aroused.
  - Vasocongestion is swelling of the genital tissues with blood.
  - Myotonia is muscle tension; causes facial grimaces, spasms in the hands and feet and the spasm of orgasm.

- 1) Excitement Phase:
  - Vasocongestion
    - causes erection in men, and
    - swells the clitoris and flattens and spreads the vaginal lips.
    - Nipples become erect in men and women.
    - Heart rate and blood pressure increase.

- 2) Plateau Phase:
  - Testes are elevated into position for ejaculation.
  - Vasocongestion
    - swells the outer part of the vagina opening in preparation for grasping the penis.
    - The clitoris withdraws beneath the clitoral hood and shortens.
  - Blood pressure continues to rise.

- 3) Orgasmic Phase:
  - Muscle contractions propel the ejaculate out of the body.
  - Orgasm in females is manifested by 3 to 15 contractions of the pelvic muscles that surround the vaginal barrel.
  - Release of sexual tension in males and females.
  - Blood pressure and heart rate reach a peak.

- 4) Resolution Phase:
  - The body returns to its unaroused state.
  - Feelings of relaxation and satisfaction.
  - Men enter a refractory period during which they cannot experience another orgasm or ejaculate.
  - Women do not undergo a refractory period.

Peering into Private Lives

- Kinsey reports: interviews with 5,300 males and 5,940 females in the U.S. between 1938 and 1949.
  - Cannot tell whether or not Kinsey's results accurately mirrored general American sexual behavior at the time.
  - Did find a positive link between education level and premarital sex.

Sexual Motivation: Surveys of Sexual Behavior

- The National Health and Social Life Survey: interviewed 3,432 people and considered subject's gender, level of education, religion and ethnicity.
  - Males report having a higher number of sex partners.

- Most people in the U.S. limit number of sexual partners to a few.
- Level of education is connected with sexual behavior.
  - Education is more liberating.
- European and African Americans have highest number of sex partners.

Sexual Dysfunctions

- They are persistent problems in becoming sexually aroused or reaching orgasms.

- Main types include:
  - Hypoactive sexual desire disorder,
  - Female sexual arousal disorder,
  - Male erectile disorder,
  - Orgasmic disorder,
  - Premature ejaculation,
  - Dyspareunia, and
  - Vaginismus.

Causes of Sexual Dysfunctions.

- Biological causes

- Physically or psychologically painful sexual experiences.

- Various factors can lead to performance anxiety.

Sex Therapy

- Sex Therapy generally focuses on:
  - Reducing performance anxiety
  - Changing self-defeating attitudes and expectations
  - Teaching sexual skills
  - Enhancing sexual knowledge
  - Improving sexual communication

Sexual Coercion: Confounding Sex and Aggression

- Sexual coercion includes rape and other forms of sexual pressure.

- It also includes any sexual activity between and adult and a child.

Rape: A Crime of Violence

- As many as 1 in 4 women in the US has been raped.

- 4 out of 5 rapes are committed by acquaintances.

Controversy in Psychology: Why do men rape women?

- Sex is not the only reason

- Many argue it is way that men express dominance over or anger toward women

- Many social critics argue that American culture also socializes men into becoming rapists

Myths about Rape

- Women frequently blamed when they are raped because

of myths
- – Most Americans above 50 believe the woman is partly responsible when dressed provocatively.
- – "Women say no when they mean yes"

Preventing Rape

- Sociocultural perspective
  - – Public examination of and challenge to widely held beliefs that contribute to rape
- Personal level.
  - – The New Our bodies, Ourselves includes helpful tips to prevent rape by strangers.
  - – Powell (1996) provides suggestions for avoiding date rape.

Sexual Harassment

- Involves deliberate or repeated unwanted comments, gestures or physical contact of a sexual nature.
- Similar to rape, society often blames the victim of sexual harassment.

Life Connections: Understanding and Preventing HIV/AIDS and other Sexually Transmitted Infections

- Psychological risk factors can be cognitive or behavioral
  - – Cognitive: people deny or underestimate their risk of infection.
  - – Behavioral: Despite their knowledge of the effects of infection, many people do not change their behavior to help prevent infection

HIV/AIDS

- AIDS is a fatal condition where person's immune system is so weakened, they are attacked by so-called opportunistic diseases
- Human Immunodeficiency virus causes AIDS.
- HIV is transmitted by infected blood, semen, vaginal and cervical secretions, and breast milk.
- HIV kills CD4 lymphocytes.
- AIDS is characterized by fatigue, fever, unexplained weight loss, swollen lymph nodes, diarrhea, and, in many cases, impairment of learning and memory.

Diagnosis and Treatment

- Generally diagnosed by means of blood, saliva, or urine tests.
- There is no safe effective vaccine, but there have been development in treatment
  - – AZT
  - – Protease Inhibitors
- Treatment is expensive and not all people with AIDS respond

Preventing HIV/AIDS and other STI's

- A-B problem: people do not always behave in accordance with their attitudes. Knowledge may not be enough to change behavior.

Prevention tips

- Don't ignore the threat.
- Remain abstinent
- Engage in monogamous relationship with uninfected person.
- Be selective.
- Inspect your partner's genitals
- Wash your genitals before and after contact.
- Use condom.
- Talk to your Doctor if you fear infection.
- When in doubt, stop.

Chapter 13: Stress, Health, and Adjustment

Health Psychology

- Studies the relationship between psychological factors and the prevention and treatment of physical health problems.
    - Psychological factors such as stress, behavior patterns and attitudes can lead to or aggravate illness.
    - People can cope with stress.
    - Stress and pathogens interact to influence the immune system.
    - People decide whether or not to seek health care.
    - Psychological forms of intervention can contribute to physical health.

Stress

- Stress is the demand made on an organism to adapt, cope, or adjust.
    - Some stress is healthful (eustress).
    - Intense of prolonged stress can harm the body.

Daily Hassles

- Daily hassles are regularly occurring conditions and experiences that can threaten or harm our well-being.

- Daily hassles and uplifts can be grouped as follows:
    - Household hassles.
    - Health hassles.
    - Time-pressure hassles.
    - Inner concern hassles.
    - Environmental hassles.
    - Financial responsibility hassles.
    - Work hassles.
    - Security hassles.

- These hassles are linked to psychological variables such as nervousness, worrying, inability to get started, feelings of sadness, and feelings of loneliness.

Life Changes

- Life changes require adjustment. Even positive ones can lead to headaches, high blood pressure, and other health problems.

- Life changes differ from daily hassles in two key ways:
    - Many life changes are positive and desirable. Hassles are negative.
    - Hassles occur regularly. Life changes occur at irregular intervals.

- Hassles, Life Changes, and Health Problems.
    - Hassles and life changes can predict health problems such as heart disease, cancer and athletic injuries.

CONTROVERSY IN PSYCHOLOGY: Just How Are Daily Hassles and Life Changes Connected With Health Problems?

- It may appear obvious that hassles and life changes

should cause health problems.

- But some researchers are not convinced that the causal connections are there.
  - Nature of the links.
  - Positive versus negative life changes.
  - Personality differences.
  - Cognitive appraisal.
- Optimism also helps people cope with the effects of stress.

Conflict

- Conflict is the feeling of being pulled in two or more directions by opposing motives.

Types of Conflict

- Approach-approach conflict.
  - The least stressful type.
  - Each of two goals is desirable and both are within reach.
- Avoidance-avoidance conflict.
  - A person is motivated to avoid each of two negative goals. Avoiding one of them requires approaching the other.
- Approach-avoidance conflict.
  - The same goal produces both approach and avoidance motives.
- Multiple approach-avoidance conflict.
  - Each of several alternative courses of action has pluses and minuses.

Irrational Beliefs

- Ellis notes that our beliefs about events as well as the events themselves can be stressors.
  - Ellis's A-B-C approach.
    - A is the activating event.
    - C is the consequence.
    - B is the belief.

The Type A Behavior Pattern

- Type A people are:
  - Highly driven
  - Competitive
  - Impatient
  - Aggressive
  - Feel rushed and under pressure
  - Find it difficult to give up control or power
  - They hold to the irrational belief that they must be perfectly competent and achieving in everything they undertake.
- Type B people in contrast are:
  - Relaxed
  - More focused on the quality of life
  - Less ambitious and less impatient.

Psychological Moderators of Stress.
Expectations affect our ability to withstand stress.

- High self-efficacy expectations are accompanied by relatively lower levels of adrenaline and noradrenaline in the bloodstream.
- People who are self-confident are less prone to be disturbed by adverse events.

- Psychological Hardiness
  - Psychological hardiness also helps people resist stress.
  - Characteristics include:
    - High in commitment.
    - High in challenge.
    - High in perceived control.
    - Hardy people are more resistant to stress because they choose to face it.

- Sense of Humor
  - Feelings of happiness may have beneficial effects on the immune system.
  - Humor can moderate the effects of stress.
  - There is a significant relationship between negative life events and stress scores.

- Predictability and Control.
  - The ability to predict a stressor apparently moderates its impact.
    - Control and even the illusion of control can moderate impact.
    - Internals:
      - people who wish to exercise control over their situations.
    - Externals:
      - people who do not wish to exercise control over their situations.

- Social Support
  - seems to act as a buffer against the effects of stress.
  - Sources of social support include:
    - Emotional concern.
    - Instrumental aid.
    - Information.
    - Appraisal.
    - Socializing.

Stress and the Body

- The General Adaptation Syndrome.
  - The general adaptation syndrome was proposed by Selye.
  - The syndrome is a cluster of bodily changes that occur in three stages:
    - Alarm
    - Resistance
    - Exhaustion

- The Alarm Reaction.
  - The alarm reaction is triggered by perception of a stressor.
  - The alarm reaction involves bodily changes that are initiated by the brain and regulated by the endocrine system and the sympathetic division of the ANS.

A Controversy in Psychology: Do Men and Women respond differently to stress?

- Females tend to "tend and befriend" which involves nurturing and seeking the support of others.

- Males more likely to withdraw from family or start arguments.

- Evolutionary Perspective.
  - Tend and Befriend promotes the survival of females who are tending to offspring.
  - Oxytocin, released during stress tends to have a calming effect.
  - This biobehavioral pattern may provide insights into why women live an average of 71/2 years longer than men.

- Other Views.
  - Differences in hormones.
  - Differences may reflect learning and culture instead of being genetically based.

- The Resistance Stage.
  - If the stressor isn't removed we enter the adaptation or resistance stage.
    - The body attempts to restore lost energy and repair bodily damage.

- The Exhaustion Stage.
  - If the stressor isn't dealt with we may enter the exhaustion stage.
  - We become exhausted if the stressor continues indefinitely.
  - The body is depleted of the resources required for combating stress.

- Stress suppresses the immune system.
  - The immune system has several functions that combat disease.
    - Production of white blood cells (leukocytes).
    - Foreign substances are called antigens.
    - Inflammation.

- Stress and the Immune System.
  - Psychoneuroimmunology is the study of the relationship among:
    - psychological factors,
    - the nervous system,
    - the endocrine system,
    - the immune system, and
    - disease.

- One of the reasons stress exhausts us is that it stimulates the production of steroids.
  - Steroids suppress the functioning of the immune system.
  - Persistent secretion of steroids decreases inflammation and interferes with the formation of antibodies.

Psychology and Health.

- Biological factors such as:
  - pathogens, inoculations, injuries, age, gender, and a family history of disease may be the most obvious cause of disease.
  - Genes only create the predisposition toward the health problem.
- Many health problems are affected by psychological factors, such as attitudes, emotions, and behavior.
- Stopping smoking, eating right, exercising and controlling alcohol use would prevent a number of types of deaths.

Headaches

- Headaches are the most common stress-related physical ailments.

Migraines

- Characterized by:
  - A sudden onset.
  - Severe throbbing pain on one side of the head.
  - May last for hours or days.
  - Visual problems.
  - Perceptual of unusual odors.
  - Sensitivity to light.
  - Loss of balance.
  - Vomiting.
  - Loss of appetite.
  - Changes in mood.
- Triggers include:
  - Barometric pressure.
  - Pollen.
  - Certain drugs.
  - Chocolate.
  - Aged cheese.
  - Beer, champagne and red wine.
  - Hormonal changes.

Coronary Heart Disease

- Coronary Heart Disease (CHD) is the leading cause of death in the United States.
  - Risk factors include:
    - Family history.
    - Physiological conditions.
    - Patterns of consumption.
    - Type A behavior.
    - Hostility and holding in feelings of anger.

- Job strain.
- Chronic fatigue and chronic emotional strain.
- Sudden stressors.
- A physically inactive lifestyle.

Cancer

- The number one killer of women in the US and number two killer of men.
- Characterized by the development of abnormal, or mutant cells that may take root anywhere in the body.
- Risk Factors.
    - People can inherit a disposition toward cancer.
    - Behaviors also contributing are:
        - Smoking.
        - Drinking alcohol.
        - Eating animal fats.
        - Sunbathing.
        - Prolonged psychological conditions such as depression.
- Stress and Cancer.
    - Once cancer has developed, stress can influence its course.

Psychological Factors in the Treatment of Cancer.

- Feelings of anxiety and depression are often found in individuals suffering with cancer.
- Psychological stress due to cancer can weaken the immune system, setting the stage for other health problems.
- Additional treatments/suggestions include:
    - Relaxation training.
    - Guided imagery.
    - Control is a factor in hardiness.
    - Patient's moods are connected with the functioning of the immune system.
    - Having a fighting spirit.

LIFE CONNECTIONS:
Preventing and Coping with Health Problems

- Methods suggested by psychologists for coping with stress include:
    - Telling yourself that you can live with another person's disappointment.
    - Taking a deep breath and telling yourself to relax.
    - Taking the scenic route to work.
    - Jogging for half an hour.
- Controlling Irrational Thoughts
    - People often feel pressure from own irrational thoughts
    - A multi-step procedure for controlling irrational thoughts include:
        - Develop awareness of the thoughts by careful self-examination.
        - Evaluate the accuracy of the thoughts.

- Prepare thoughts that are incompatible with the irrational.
- Reward yourself with a mental pat on the back.

- Lowering Arousal:
  - Stress tends to trigger intense activity in the sympathetic branch of the ANS.
  - Arousal is a sign that something may be wrong.
  - Tools that help include:
    - Meditation.
    - Biofeedback.
    - Progressive relaxation.

- 10 steps of meditation.
  - Begin by meditating once or twice a day for 10-20 minutes.
  - In meditation what you don't do is more important than what you do do.
  - Create a quiet, nondisruptive environment.
  - Do not eat for an hour beforehand.
  - Assume a comfortable position.
  - As a device to aid in concentrating, focus on your breathing.
  - If you are using a mantra prepare by saying the mantra out loud several times.
  - If disruptive thoughts enter your mind don't allow them to pass through.
  - Allow yourself to drift.
  - Above all, take what you can get.

- Exercising
  - Exercising, particularly aerobic exercise, enhances the functioning of the immune system, contributes to our psychological well-being, and helps us cope with stress.
  - Aerobic exercise refers to exercise that requires a sustained increase in consumption of oxygen.
  - Anaerobic exercise involves short bursts of muscle activity.
  - Sustained physical activity reduces hypertension, the risk of heart attacks and strokes.

- Reducing the risk of CHD through Behavior Modification
  - Stopping smoking
  - Controlling weight.
  - Reducing hypertension.
  - Lowering cholesterol.
  - Modifying Type A behavior.
  - Managing feelings of Anger.
  - Exercising.

- Preventing and Coping with Headaches.
  - Suggestions for preventing headaches.
    - Challenging irrational beliefs.
    - Exercising.
    - Meditation.
    - Progressive relaxation.
    - Biofeedback training.

- Preventing and Coping with Cancer.
  - Suggestions include:
    - Limit exposure to behavioral risk factors.
    - Modify diet.
    - Exercise regularly.
    - Have regular medical checkups.
    - Regulate exposure to stress.
    - If struck with cancer, fight it energetically.

_____

_____

_____

Chapter 14: Psychological Disorders

Historic Views of Psychological Disorders

- In the past people believed that psychological disorders were caused by possession by the Devil.
  - People attributed unusual behavior and psychological disorders to demons.
  - The Hammer of Witches.

What Are Psychological Disorders?

- Psychological disorders are behaviors or mental processes that are connected with various kinds of distress or disability.

- Disorders are characterized on the following criteria:
  - They are unusual.
  - They suggest faulty perception or interpretation of reality.
    - Hearing voices, seeing things, hallucinations, ideas of persecution.
  - They suggest severe personal distress.
  - They are self-defeating.
  - They are dangerous.
  - The individual's behavior is socially unacceptable.

Classifying Psychological Disorders.

- The most widely used classification scheme for psychological disorders is the Diagnostic and Statistical Manual (DSM) of the American Psychiatric Association.

- Thomas Szasz believes that disorders are really just problems in living rather than disorders.
  - Labeling people degrades them, encourages them to evade their personal and social responsibilities.
  - Labeling people as sick accords too much power to health professionals.
  - Troubled people need to be encouraged to take greater responsibility for solving their own problems.

CONTROVERSY IN PSYCHOLOGY: Is a Gay Male or Lesbian Sexual Orientation A Psychological Disorder?

- Until 1973 a gay male or lesbian sexual orientation was considered to be a psychological disorder.
  - A category for people who are distressed about their sexual orientation remains in place.

- Gay males and lesbians are more likely than heterosexuals to experience feelings of anxiety and depression and they are more prone to suicide.

- Bailey proposed interpretations of the issues surrounding homosexuality:
  - Societal oppression causes the higher incidence of depression and suicidality.

- Homosexuality reflects a departure from typical development.
- Sexual orientation reflects prenatal sex hormones.
- Homosexual people could reflect differences in lifestyle.

Anxiety Disorders

- Anxiety has psychological and physical features.
  - Psychological features include:
    - Worrying.
    - Fear of the worst things happening.
    - Fear of losing control.
    - Nervousness.
    - Inability to relax.
  - Physical features include:
    - Arousal of the sympathetic branch of the autonomic nervous system:
      - Trembling.
      - Sweating.
      - Pounding heart.
      - Elevated blood pressure.
      - Faintness.

- Phobias.
  - Specific phobias are excessive, irrational fears of specific objects or situations, such as snakes or heights.
  - Social phobias are persistent fears of scrutiny by others or of doing something that will be humiliating or embarrassing.
    - Agoraphobia: fear of being out in open, busy areas.

- Panic Disorder is an abrupt attack of acute anxiety that is not triggered by a specific object or situation.

- Generalized Anxiety Disorder is persistent anxiety that cannot be attributed to a phobic object, situation or activity. It seems to be free-floating.

- Obsessive-Compulsive Disorder.
  - Obsessions are recurrent, anxiety provoking thoughts or images that seem irrational and disrupt daily life.
  - Compulsions are thought or behaviors that tend to reduce the anxiety connected with obsessions.

- Stress Disorders.
  - Posttraumatic stress disorder (PTSD) is characterized by a rapid heart rate and feelings of anxiety and helplessness that are caused by a traumatic experience.
  - Acute stress disorder is characterized by feelings of anxiety and helplessness that are caused by a traumatic event.
    - Acute stress disorder occurs within a month of the event and lasts from 2 days to 4 weeks.

Theoretical Views

- Psychological views.

- Psychodynamic:
  - Phobias symbolize conflicts originating in childhood.
  - Generalized anxiety as persistent difficulty in repressing primitive impulses.
  - Obsessions are explained as leakage of unconscious impulses.
- Learning theorists:
  - Phobias are conditioned fears that were acquired in childhood. Observational learning also plays a role.
- Cognitive theorists:
  - Anxiety is maintained by thinking that one is in a terrible situation and helpless to change it.
- Biological Views.
  - Anxiety tends to run in families.
    - Twin studies show a higher concordance rate for anxiety disorders among identical twins than among fraternal twins.
  - Mineka (2001) suggest that humans are genetically predisposed to fear stimuli that may have posed a threat to their ancestors.
  - The brain may not be sensitive enough to GABA, a neurotransmitter that may help calm anxiety reactions.

Dissociative Disorders

- Dissociative disorders are characterized by a separation of mental processes such as thoughts, emotions, identity, memory, or consciousness.

Types of Dissociative Disorders

- Dissociative amnesia
  - characterized by the person suddenly being unable to recall important personal information.

- Dissociative Fugue
  - characterized by the person abruptly leaving their home or place of work and traveling to another place, having lost all memory of their past. The new personality is often more outgoing than the less inhibited one.

- Dissociative identity disorder (formerly termed multiple personality disorder)
  - characterized by two or more identities or personalities, each with distinct traits and memories, occupying the same person. Each identity may or may not be aware of the others.

Theoretical Views

- Psychodynamic theory
  - explains this as massive repression.

- Learning theorists
  - suggest that people have learned not to think about bad memories or disturbing impulses in order to avoid

feelings of anxiety, guilt or shame.

Somatoform Disorders

* Somatoform disorders are characterized by physical problems in people, such as paralysis, pain, or a persistent belief that they have a serious disease. Yet no evidence of a physical abnormality can be found.

Types of somatoform disorders

* Conversion disorder
  - characterized by a major change in, or loss of, physical functioning although there are no medical findings to explain the loss of functioning.
    * The person is not faking as they seem to be converting a source of stress into a physical difficulty.

* Hypochondriasis
  - characterized by people insisting that they are suffering with a serious physical illness even though no medical evidence of illness can be found.

* Theoretical Views.
  - There is research evidence that people who develop hypochondriasis are particularly sensitive to bodily sensations and tend to ruminate about them.

CONTROVERSY IN PSYCHOLOGY: Are somatoform disorders the special province of women?
Hippocrates believed that hysteria was caused by a wandering uterus.

* Psychodynamic view suggests that conversion disorders protect the individual from feelings of guilt, shame or from another source of stress.

* Conversion disorders are not the special province of women.

Mood Disorders

* Mood disorders are characterized by disturbance in expressed emotions generally involving sadness or elation.

Types of Mood Disorders.

* Major depression
  * the common cold of psychological problems.

The Case of Women and Depression.
Women are about two times more likely to be diagnosed with depression than men.
  - Low levels of estrogen have been suggested as a reason.
    * Hormonal changes, menstrual cycle, and childbirth may contribute to depression in women.

* Women are more likely to admit to depression.

* Women are more likely to ruminate about stresses.

* A panel convened by the APA attributed most of the

gender difference to the greater stresses placed on women.
  - Multiple demands including:
    * Demands of childbearing.
    * Child rearing.
    * Financial support of the family.
* Women are more likely to have experienced physical and sexual abuse, poverty, single parenthood, and sexism.
* Women are more likely to help other people which heaps additional care giving burdens on themselves.

Types of Mood Disorders.

* Bipolar Disorder
  - formerly known as manic-depressive disorder and is characterized by:
    * Mood swings from ecstatic elation to deep depression.

Theoretical Views

* Depression may be a reaction to losses and stress.
  - We tend to be depressed by things we bring on ourselves.
* Psychological Views:
  - Psychoanalysts suggest that anger is turned inward.
    * Bipolar disorder may be seen as the personality being dominated by the superego and then by the ego.
* Learning theorists suggest that depressed people behave as though they cannot obtain reinforcement.
  - They have an external locus of control.
  - Researchers have found links between depression and learned helplessness.
* Cognitive factors contributing to depression include making irrational demands on themselves.
  - Depressed people tend to ruminate about feelings of depression.
  - Attribution styles include: internal vs. external; stable vs. unstable; and global vs. specific.
* Biological Factors.
  - Depression is heritable.
  - Genetic factors appear to be involved.
    * Bipolar disorder may be connected with genetic material found on Chromosome 18.
  - Depression research focuses on the underutilization of the neurotransmitter serotonin in the brain.

Schizophrenia

* Schizophrenia is a severe psychological disorder that touches every aspect of a person's life.
* Characterized by:
  - Disturbances in:

- thought and language.
- perception and attention.
- motor activity and mood.
  - Withdrawal and absorption in daydreams or fantasy.
  - Jumbled speech.
  - Delusions.
  - Hallucinations.
  - Stupors: slow motor activity.
  - Emotional responses that may be flat.

Types of Schizophrenia

- Paranoid type
- Disorganized type show
- Catatonic type

Theoretical Views

- Psychological views:
  - Psychodynamic perspective suggests that the ego is overwhelmed by sexual or aggressive impulses from the id.
  - Learning theorists explain schizophrenia in terms of conditioning and observational learning.
  - Some researchers are interested in the connections between psychosocial stressors and biological factors.
- Biological Views:
  - Schizophrenia appears to be a brain disorder.
  - Size of the ventricles in the brain.
  - Activity levels in the brain.
  - Brain chemistry.

Possible causes of Schizophrenia

- Heredity.
  - Chromosome 1.
- Complications during pregnancy.
- Birth during winter.
- Poor maternal nutrition.
- Atypical development of the central nervous system.
- The Dopamine theory of schizophrenia suggests that people with schizophrenia overutilize dopamine.
  - They may have larger numbers of dopamine receptors.
- The multifactorial model suggests that genetic factors create a predisposition toward schizophrenia. Then other factors contribute to the cause of the disorder.

CONTROVERSY IN PSYCHOLOGY:
Should we ban the insanity plea?

- The issue is competence to stand trial.
- M'Naghten rule states that the accused did not understand what they were doing at the time of the act, did not realize it was wrong, or was succumbing to an

irresistible impulse.

- Although the public estimates that the insanity defense is used in about 37% of felony cases, it is actually raised in only 1%.
  - People found not guilty by reason of insanity are institutionalized for indefinite terms.

Personality Disorders

- Personality disorders
  - characterized by enduring patterns of behavior that are inflexible, and maladaptive.
  - These behaviors typically impair social or personal functioning and are a source of distress to the individual or to other people.

Types of Personality Disorders

- Paranoid personality disorder
  - tendency to interpret other people's behavior as threatening or demeaning.
- Schizotypal personality disorder is characterized by peculiarities of thought, perception, or behavior such as excessive fantasy and suspiciousness, feelings of being unreal, or odd usage of words.
- Schizoid personality is defined by indifference to relationships and flat emotional response.
  - People with this disorder are loners.
- Antisocial personality disorder
  - is characterized by persistently violating the rights of others and being in conflict with the law.
- Borderline personality disorder
  - Is characterized by instability in relationships, self-image, and mood, and lack of impulse control
- Avoidant personality disorder
  - individuals are generally unwilling to enter a relationship without some assurance of acceptance because they fear rejection and criticism.

Theoretical Views.
Freudian model
  - suggests that there are problems in the Oedipus complex. The superego does not develop.
- Learning theorists
  - suggest that childhood experiences can contribute to maladaptive ways of relating to others in adulthood.
- Personality traits are to some degree heritable.
- There is some evidence that those with antisocial personality disorder have less gray matter in the prefrontal cortex of the brain.

LIFE CONNECTIONS: Understanding and Preventing Suicide.

- About 30,000 people each year take their lives in the U.S.
- Risk Factors in Suicide:
  - Linked to feelings of depression and hopelessness.
  - Highly achieving.
  - Rigid perfectionists.
  - Set impossibly high expectations for themselves.
  - Compare themselves negatively with others.
  - Suicidal Adolescents experience four psychological problems:
    - Confusion about self.
    - Impulsiveness.
    - Emotional instability.
    - Interpersonal problems.
  - Suicide attempts are more common following stressful life events.
    - Exit events are events that entail a loss of social support.
  - People who consider suicide are less capable of solving problems.
  - Suicide tends to run in families.
- Ethnicity:
  - 17% of Native Americans has attempted suicide.
  - African Americans are least likely to attempt suicide (6.5%).
  - European Americans at 8%.
  - Latino Americans are at 1 in 8.
- Gender:
  - About three times as many females as males attempt suicide; but about five times as many males succeed.
- Myths about Suicide.
  - Most people who commit suicide give warnings about their intentions, they aren't just seeking attention.
  - Many people who commit suicide have made prior attempts.
  - Discussing suicide with a person does not prompt the person to attempt suicide.
  - Suicidal thinking is not necessarily a sign of psychosis, neurosis, or a personality disorder.
- Some Warning Signs of Suicide:
  - Changes in eating and sleeping patterns.
  - Difficulty concentrating on school work.
  - A sharp decline in school performance and attendance.
  - Loss of interest in previously enjoyed activities.
  - Giving away prized possessions.
  - Complaints about physical problems when no medical basis for the problem can be found.
  - Withdrawal from social relationships.
  - Personality or mood changes.
  - Talking or writing about death or dying.
  - abuse of drugs or alcohol
  - An attempted suicide.
- Some Things You What Can You Do?
  - Keep talking. Encourage the person to talk.

- Be a good listener.
- Suggest that something other than suicide might solve the problem.
- Emphasize as concretely as possible how the person's suicide would be devastating to you and to other people who care.
- Ask how the person intends to commit suicide. Individuals with a concrete plan are at a greater risk.

_____

_____

_____

_____

_____

_____

Chapter 15: Methods of Therapy

What is Therapy?

- Psychotherapy:
  - a systematic interaction between a therapist and a client that:
  - Applies psychological principles to affect the client's thoughts, feelings, or behavior in order to;
    - Help the client overcome psychological disorders,
    - Adjust to problems in living,
    - Or develop as an individual.

The History of Therapies

- Treatments often reflected demonological thinking.
- Asylums built for warehousing not treatment.
- Humanitarian reform began in:
  - Paris with Philippe Pinel at the La Bicetre hospital.
  - England with William Tuke.
  - America with Dorothea Dix.
- Mental Hospitals: gradually began replacing asylums.
  - In the mid 1950s more than a million people resided in facilities.
- The Community Mental Health Movement:
  - attempt to maintain new patients as outpatients and to serve patients who have been released from mental hospitals.

Psychodynamic Therapies

- Based on the thinking of Freud.
  - Assume that psychological disorders reflect early childhood experiences and internal conflicts.
- Traditional Psychoanalysis
  - Psychoanalysis can extend for months, even years.
  - The aim is to provide insight into the conflicts that are the cause of the person's problems.
  - Catharsis is a spilling forth of repressed conflicts and guilt.

Traditional Psychoanalysis

- Free Association.
  - Hypnosis allowed clients to focus on repressed conflicts.
  - Free association: the client is made comfortable and asked to talk about anything that comes to mind.
- Resistance:
  - clients may not talk about threatening ideas. These ideas are repressed.
- Interpretation:
  - the process of showing the client how revealed ideas illustrate deep seated feelings and conflicts.

- Transference:
  - clients respond to the therapist with the attitudes and feelings they have toward other people in their lives.
  - Often clients reenact their childhood conflicts.
- Dream Analysis.
  - Freud believed that dreams were the royal road to the unconscious.
    - Dreams are determined by unconscious processes as well as the events of the day.
    - Unconscious impulses are expressed in dreams as a form of wish fulfillment.
    - Perceived dream content is called the manifest content.
    - The hidden or symbolic content is called the latent content.

Psychodynamic Therapies: Modern Approaches

- The modern approach is:
  - Briefer and less intense.
  - Focus on revealing unconscious material.
  - Client and therapist usually sit face to face rather than having the client lie on a couch.
  - The therapist is usually directive.
  - Usually more focus on the ego and less emphasis on the Id.

Humanistic-Existential Therapies

- The focus is on quality of the client's subjective, conscious experience.
  - Focus on the here and now.
- Client-Centered Therapy: Removing Roadblocks to Self Actualization.
  - Client centered therapy is intended to help people get in touch with their genuine feelings and pursue their own interests, regardless of other people's wishes.
  - Clients are free to make choices and control our destinies.
  - Psychological problems arise from roadblocks placed in the path of self-actualization.
    - Client centered therapy is non-directive and focuses on helping the person feel whole.
- Gestalt Therapy
  - Gestalt therapy was originated by Fritz Perls.
  - The approach assumes that people disown parts of themselves and don social masks.
  - The goal is to integrate conflicting parts of their personality.
  - Gestalt therapy is highly directive.

Behavior Therapy

- Applies the principles of learning to directly promote desired behavioral change.
- Fear-Reduction Methods.
    - The client learns to handle increasingly disturbing

stimuli while anxiety is being counterconditioned.
- Modeling relies on observational learning.
  - Clients model individuals dealing with the feared object.
- Aversive Conditioning.
  - Controversial procedure in which painful or aversive stimuli are paired with unwanted impulses.
- Operant Conditioning Procedures.
  - We tend to repeat behavior that is reinforced.
  - Behavior that is not reinforced tends to become extinguished.

Operant Conditioning
- The Token Economy.
  - Patients must use tokens to purchase things they like.
  - Tokens are reinforcements for productive activities.
- Successive Approximations.
  - Successive approximations is often used to help clients build good habits.
- Social Skills Training.
  - Employ self monitoring, coaching, modeling, role playing, behavioral rehearsal and feedback.
- Biofeedback Training.
  - Help clients become more aware of, and gain control over, various bodily functions.
- Self Control Methods.
  - Functional Analysis of Behavior.
    - Functional analysis of problem behaviors which helps determine stimuli that trigger behaviors and reinforcers that maintain them.
    - Clients are taught to manipulate the antecedents and consequences of their behavior.

Cognitive Therapies
- Cognitive therapy focuses on changing the beliefs, attitudes and automatic types of thinking that create and compound their client's problems.
  - Heighten insight into current cognitions.
  - Appraisals of unfortunate events can heighten our discomfort and impair our coping ability.
  - Therapists need to challenge beliefs that are not supported by evidence.
    - Clients need to become personal scientists and challenge beliefs that are not supported by evidence.

- Rational Emotive Behavior Therapy
  - focuses on beliefs about events as well as the events.
  - Many harbor irrational beliefs.
    - The irrational belief that we must have the love and approval of people who are important to us.

- The irrational belief that we must prove ourselves to be thoroughly competent, adequate, and achieving.
- The methods are directive and active.

Group Therapies

- Advantages to group therapies:
  - It is economical.
  - Provides more information and life experience for clients to draw on.
  - Appropriate behavior receives group support.
  - Affiliating with people with similar problems is reassuring.
  - Group members provide hope for other members.
  - Many clients practice social skills in a relatively non-threatening atmosphere.

Types of Groups

- Encounter Groups.
- Couple Therapy.
- Family Therapy.
  -

Does psychotherapy work?

- In 1952 Hans Eysenck published a review of psychotherapy research and determined that the rate of improvement among people in psychotherapy was no greater than the rate of spontaneous remission.
- Meta-analysis (statistical averaging) is now used and shows that psychotherapy is effective.

Problems in Conducting Research on Psychotherapy

- Problems in Running Experiments on Psychotherapy.
  - The ideal method for evaluating treatment is the experiment.
    - Experiments in therapy are difficult to arrange and control.
    - Is it ethical to leave clients in the control condition?
    - Difficult to have blind and double blind studies.
- Problems in Measuring Outcomes of Therapy.
  - Cannot directly measure some qualities (self actualization, insight, etc.)
- Are Clinical Judgments Valid?
  - Many clinicians believe that important clinical questions cannot be answered through research.
  - Therapists have a stake in believing their clients benefit from treatment.
- Does Therapy Help Because of the Method or Because of "Nonspecific Factors"?
  - Nonspecific factors are other factors besides therapy that may contribute to recovery. They may include:
    - The client's relationship with the therapist.

- Clients present themselves in a positive light.
- What is the Experimental Treatment in Psychotherapy Outcome Studies?
  - It is difficult to specify just what is happening in the therapeutic session.

Analysis of the Effectiveness of Therapy

- Smith and Glass found that:
  - Psychodynamic and client-centered are most effective with well educated, verbal, strongly motivated clients.
  - Gestalt therapy wasn't as effective.

- Shadish found that:
  - Psychotherapy is generally effective.
  - The more therapy the better.
  - Therapy is more effective when the outcome measures reflect the treatment.

- It is not enough to ask which type of therapy is most effective.
  - We must ask which type is most effective for a particular problem and a particular patient.

Biological Therapies

- Biological therapies apply what is known of people's biological structures and processes to the amelioration of psychological disorders.

- Drug Therapy:
  - Antianxiety drugs.
    - Valium is usually prescribed for patients who complain of generalized anxiety or panic attacks.

- Antipsychotic Drugs.
  - reduce agitation, delusions, and hallucinations.
    - Clozaril acts by blocking dopamine receptors in the brain.

- Antidepressants.
  - used to help clients with eating disorders, panic attacks, obsessive-compulsive disorders and social phobia.
  - Antidepressants work by increasing levels of neurotransmitters.
  - Monoamine oxidase (MAO) inhibitors block the activity of an enzyme that breaks down noradrenaline and serotonin.
  - Tricyclic antidepressants prevent the reuptake of noradrenaline and serotonin.
  - Serotonin-reuptake inhibitors (Prozac) block reuptake of serotonin.
  - Usually takes weeks to build up to therapeutic levels.

- Lithium.
  - Lithium is used to flatten out cycles of manic behavior and depression.
  - Affects the functioning of neurotransmitters, including glutamate.

- Electroconvulsive Therapy.

    – Used mainly for people with major depression who do not respond to antidepressants.

CONTROVERSY IN PSYCHOLOGY:
Should health professionals use electroconvulsive therapy?

- Side effects of ECT include:
  - Memory problems.
  - Though the effects may be temporary.

Psychosurgery

- Prefrontal lobotomy: a pick like instrument severs the nerve pathways that link the prefrontal lobes of the brain to the thalamus.
  - Egas Moniz brought the procedure to the U.S. in the 1930s.
  - This method has been largely discontinued in the U.S.

Does Biological Therapy Work?

- Drug therapy has helped many people with severe psychological disorders.

- The combination of cognitive therapy and antidepressants is superior to either treatment alone with chronically depressed people.

LIFE CONNECTIONS:
Alleviating Depression

- To reverse the characteristics of depression try:
  - Engaging in pleasant events.
    - There is a relationship between our moods and what we do.
    - One may be able to use pleasant events to lift mood purposefully.
  - Thinking rationally.
    - People tend to:
      - Internalize blame.
      - See problems as stable and global.
      - Catastrophize problems.
      - Minimize accomplishment.
  - Exercising
- Asserting yourself.
  - Nonassertive behavior patterns are linked to feelings of depression.
  - Learning to express feelings and relate to others has been shown to alleviate feelings of depression.
    -

Chapter 16: Social Psychology

Social Psychology: Individuals Among Others.

- The ways in which the environment influences behavior and mental processes.
  - Social psychology studies the nature and causes of behavior and mental processes in social situations.

- Topics covered in social psychology include: attitudes, conformity, persuasion, social perception, environmental psychology, interpersonal attraction, social influence, group conformity, and obedience.

Attitudes

- Attitudes are comprised of:
  - Cognitive evaluations.
  - Feelings.
  - Behavioral tendencies.
  - Attitudes are behavioral and cognitive tendencies that are expressed by evaluating particular people, places, or things with favor or disfavor.
  - Attitudes are learned, and they affect behavior.

A-B Problem

- The definition of attitude implies that our behavior is consistent with our cognitions.
  - The links between attitudes (A) and behaviors (B) tend to be weak to moderate.

- A number of factors influence the likelihood what we can predict behavior from attitudes:
  - Specificity: We can better predict specific behavior from specific attitudes than from global attitudes.
  - Strength of attitudes.
  - Vested interest.
  - Accessibility: brought easily to mind.

Attitudes

- Origins of Attitudes.
  - Attitudes are learned or derived from cognitive processes.
  - Conditioning may play a role in acquiring attitudes.
  - Attitudes can be acquired by observing others.
  - Cognitive Appraisal.

- Changing Attitudes Through Persuasion.
  - The elaboration likelihood model describes the ways in which people respond to persuasive messages.
    - The first (central) route inspires thoughtful considerations of arguments and evidence.
    - The second (peripheral) route associates objects with positive or negative cues.
    - The three peripheral factors are:
      - The messenger.
      - The context of the message.

- – The audience.
- The Persuasive Message
  - – Research suggests that familiarity breeds content, not contempt.
  - – Forewarning creates a kind of psychological immunity.
  - – Product claims that admit their product's weak points in addition to highlighting its strength are most believable.
  - – Fear appeal seems to work.
- The Persuasive Communicator
  - – Persuasive communicators are characterized by expertise, trustworthiness, attractiveness, or similarity to their audience.
  - – Selective avoidance and selective exposure.
    - • People tend to seek communicators whose outlook coincides with their own.
- The Context of the Message
  - – When we are in a good mood, we apparently are less likely to evaluate the situation carefully.
  - – Agreement and praise are more effective ways to encourage others to embrace your views.
- The Persuaded Audience.
  - – People with high self-esteem and low social anxiety are more likely to resist social pressure.
- The Foot-in-the-Door Technique.
  - – Research suggests that people who accede to small requests become more amenable to larger ones for a variety of reasons.

Cognitive-Dissonance Theory

- People are thinking creatures who seek consistency in their behaviors and their attitudes
- Effort Justification motivated by discomfort of cognitive dissonance

Social Perception

- Factors that contribute to social perception include:
  - – Primacy and Recency Effects
  - – Attribution Theory
- Dispositional and Situational Attributions.
  - – Dispositional attributions ascribe a person's behavior to internal factors such as personality traits and free will.
  - – Situational attributions attribute a person's actions to external factors such as social influence or socialization.
- The Fundamental Attribution Error.
  - – In cultures that view the self as independent, people tend to attribute other people's behavior primarily to internal factors such as personality traits, attitudes, and free will.
- The Actor-Observer Effect.
  - – The tendency to attribute other people's behavior to dispositional factors and our own behavior to

situational influences.

- The Self-serving Bias.
  - people are likely to ascribe their successes to internal, dispositional factors but their failures to external, situational influences.
  - There are exceptions to the self-serving bias:
    - When we work in groups we tend to take credit for the group's success but to pin the blame for failure on someone else.
    - Depressed people are more likely to ascribe their failures to internal factors, even when external factors are mostly to blame.
    - Gender bias: Men are more likely to interpret a woman's smile or friendliness toward a man as flirting.
- Body language is nonverbal language; it refers to the meanings we infer from the ways in which people carry themselves and the gestures they make.
  - Touching

  - Gazing and Staring

Social Influence

- Social influence focuses on ways in which people alter the thoughts, feelings and behaviors of others.
  - Obedience to Authority: The Milgram Studies

- Why Did People in the Milgram Study Obey the Experimenters?
  - Socialization:
  - Lack of social comparison.
  - Perception of legitimate authority.
  - The foot-in-the-door technique.
  - Inaccessibility of values.
  - Buffers in the experiment.

- Conformity: We conform when we change our behavior in order to adhere to social norms.
  - Social norms are widely accepted expectations concerning social behavior.

- The Asch Study.
  - One subject and the rest are confederates. Does the subject conform to the group though they are obviously wrong?

- Factors That Influence Conformity:
  - Belonging to a collectivist rather than an individualist society.
  - The desire to be liked by other members of the group.
  - Low self-esteem.
  - Social shyness.
  - Lack of familiarity with the task.

Group Behavior

- Social Facilitation
  - the effects on performance that result from the presence of others.

- Social loafing
  - impaired performance because of the group.
    - Diffusion of responsibility: each person may feel less obligated to help because others are present.
- Group Decision Making
  - Social decision schemes are rules that govern much of group decision making.
- Group Decision Making
  - Polarization and the "Risky Shift".
    - Polarization: is the group effect of taking an extreme position.
    - Groups tend to take greater risks than those their members would take as individuals.
- Groupthink:
  - members tend to be more influenced by group cohesiveness and a dynamic leader than by the realities of the situation.
- Mob Behavior and Deindividuation
  - Deindividuation is a state of reduced self-awareness and lowered concern for social evaluation.

Altruism and the Bystander Effect

- Altruism is selfless concern for the welfare of others.
  - Many factors contribute to helping behavior:
    - Observers are more likely to help when they are in a good mood.
    - People who are empathic are more likely to help people in need.
    - Bystanders may not help unless they believe that an emergency exists.
    - Observers must assume the responsibility to act.
    - Observers must know what to do.
    - Observers are more likely to help people they know.
    - Observers are more likely to help people who are similar to themselves.
- Altruism is selfless concern for the welfare of others.
  - The Victim: Who Is Helped?
    - Traditional gender roles persist strongly in the South.
    - Attractive and unaccompanied women are most likely to be helped by men.

Environmental Psychology

- Studies the ways in which people and the physical environment influence each other.

Noise

- High noise levels are stressful and can lead to problems: hypertension, neurological and intestinal disorders
- Loud noises reduces helping behavior.

- Sudden noises can prompt aggressive behavior.

Temperature

- Small changes in temperature (arousal) get our attention, motivate us, increase feelings of attraction, facilitate performance tasks.
- Large changes in temperature can sap our ability to cope.

Of Aromas and Air Pollution.

- Carbon Monoxide decreases oxygen-carrying capacity of the blood.
  - Impairs learning ability and perception of passage of time.

Crowding and Personal Space

- Psychological Moderators of the Impact of High Density
  - Sense of control enhances psychological hardiness.

Some Effects of City Life

- City dwellers experience stimulus overload:
  - Less willing to shake hands with, make eye contact with or help strangers.
- Cross-cultural differences do exist.

Personal Space

- Invisible boundary that serves both protective and communicative functions.
- Cross-cultural differences in definitions of personal space.

LIFE CONNECTIONS:
Understanding and Combating Prejudice.

- Prejudice is an attitude toward a group that leads people to evaluate members of that group negatively-even though they have never met them.
  - Cognitively, prejudice is linked to expectations that members of the target group will behave poorly.
  - Emotionally, prejudice is associated with negative feelings such as fear, dislike, or hatred.
  - Behaviorally, prejudice is connected with avoidance, aggression and discrimination.
  - Discrimination: negative behavior that results from prejudice.
- Stereotypes: are prejudices about certain groups that lead people to view members of those groups in a biased fashion.
  - Some stereotypes are positive rather than negative.
- Sources of Prejudice include:
  - Dissimilarity.
  - Social conflict.
  - Social learning.
  - Information processing.
  - Social categorization.
- Combating Prejudice.

- Encourage intergroup contact and cooperation.
- Present examples of admired individuals within groups that are often stigmatized.
- Attack discriminatory behavior.
- Hold discussion forums.
- Examine your own beliefs.

_____

_____

PowerVisual 1
The Scientific Method
Fill in the diagram with the appropriate terms on the right.

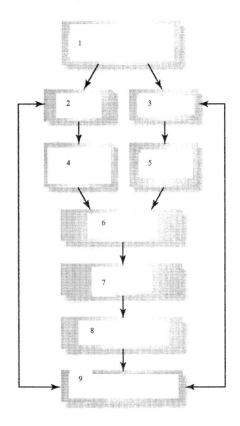

Hypothesis

Theory construction or modification

New research questions or hypothesis

Examining the research questions

Psychological theory
Daily experiences
Commonly held beliefs

Drawing conclusions

Hypothesis testing

Evidence (observation)

Research questions

Notes:

_____

_____

_____

_____

_____

_____

_____

_____

PowerVisual 2
Neurons and the Neural Impulse
Fill in the diagram with the appropriate terms on the right.

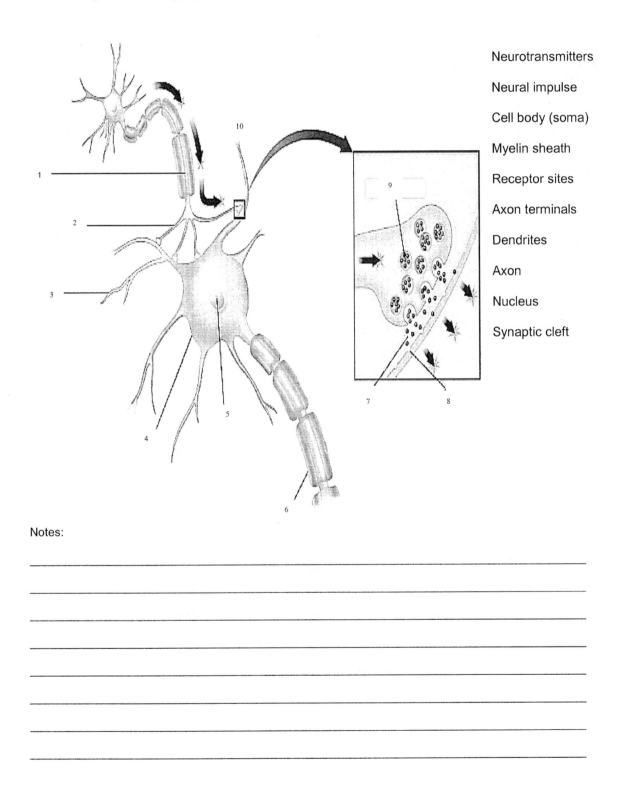

Neurotransmitters

Neural impulse

Cell body (soma)

Myelin sheath

Receptor sites

Axon terminals

Dendrites

Axon

Nucleus

Synaptic cleft

Notes:

_____

_____

_____

_____

_____

_____

_____

_____

PowerVisual 3
The Divisions of the Nervous System
Fill in the diagram with the appropriate terms on the right.

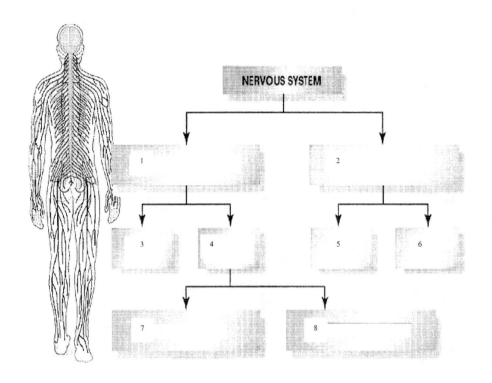

Peripheral nervous system

Central nervous system

Autonomic system

Somatic system

Parasympathetic system

Brain

Spinal cord

Sympathetic system

Notes:

_____

_____

_____

_____

_____

_____

_____

_____

_____

_____

_____

_____

PowerVisual 4
The Branches of the Autonomic Nervous System (ANS)
Fill in the diagram with the appropriate terms on the right.

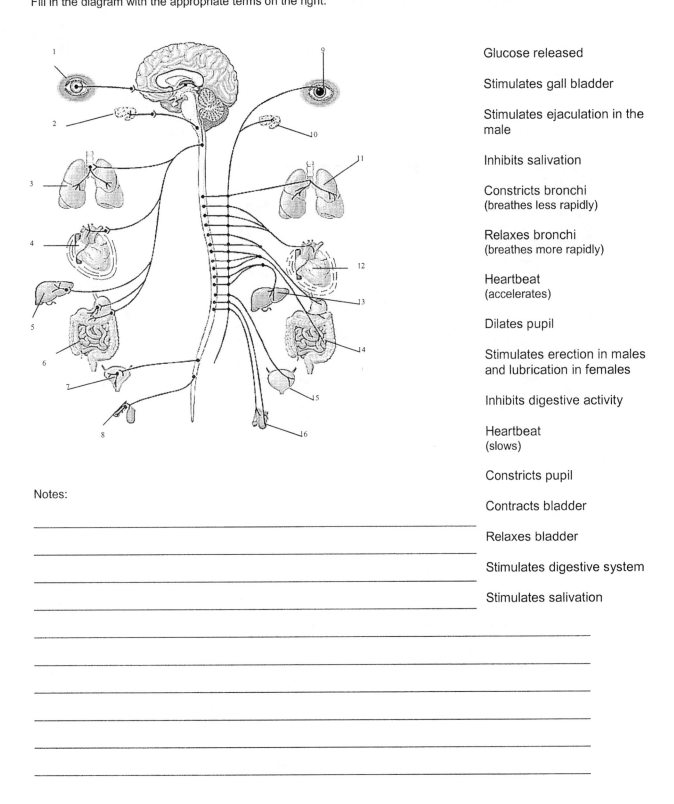

Glucose released

Stimulates gall bladder

Stimulates ejaculation in the male

Inhibits salivation

Constricts bronchi
(breathes less rapidly)

Relaxes bronchi
(breathes more rapidly)

Heartbeat
(accelerates)

Dilates pupil

Stimulates erection in males and lubrication in females

Inhibits digestive activity

Heartbeat
(slows)

Constricts pupil

Contracts bladder

Relaxes bladder

Stimulates digestive system

Stimulates salivation

Notes:

_____

_____

_____

_____

_____

_____

_____

_____

_____

PowerVisual 5
Comparing Brain Structure
Fill in the diagram with the appropriate terms on the right.

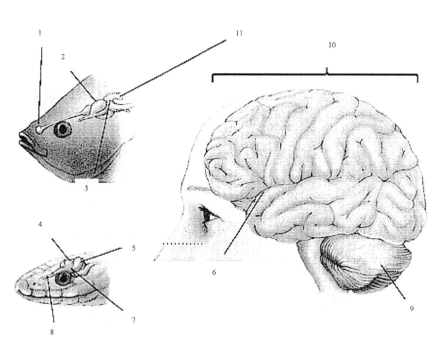

Fish Cerebellum

Reptile Neocortex

Human Neocortex

Fish Cerebrum

Reptile Olfactory Lobe

Human Cerebellum

Fish Olfactory Lobe

Reptile Cerebellum

Human Cerebrum

Fish Cortex

Reptile Cerebrum

Notes:

_____

_____

_____

_____

_____

_____

_____

_____

PowerVisual 6
The Parts of the Human Brain
Fill in the diagram with the appropriate terms on the right.

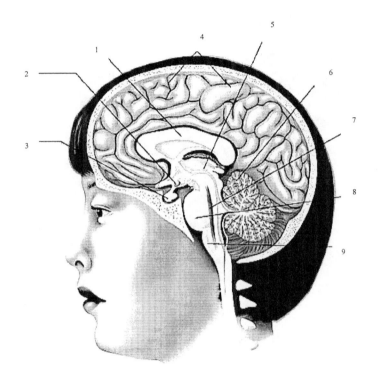

Thalamus

Hypothalamus

Medulla

Corpus Callosum

Reticular activating system

Pituitary gland

Cerebellum

Cerebrum

Pons

Notes:

_____

_____

_____

_____

_____

_____

_____

_____

_____

_____

PowerVisual 7
The Limbic System
Fill in the diagram with the appropriate terms on the right.

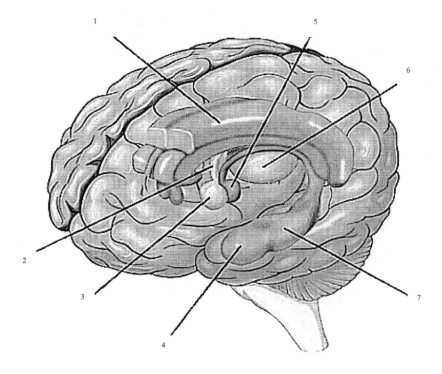

Amygdala

Thalamus

Cingulate Gyrus

Mammilliary body

Fornix

Hippocampus

Hypothalamus

Notes:

_____

_____

_____

_____

_____

_____

_____

_____

_____

_____

_____

PowerVisual 8
The Endocrine System
Fill in the diagram with the appropriate terms on the right.

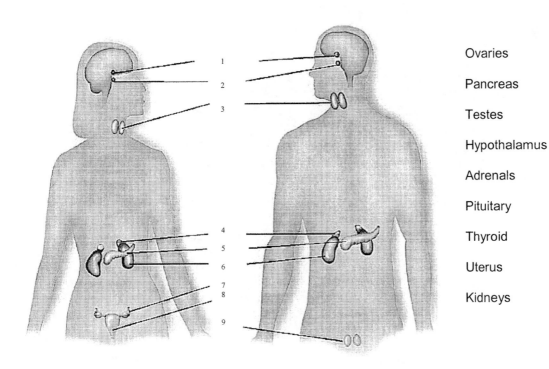

Ovaries

Pancreas

Testes

Hypothalamus

Adrenals

Pituitary

Thyroid

Uterus

Kidneys

Notes:

_____

_____

_____

_____

_____

_____

_____

_____

_____

_____

PowerVisual 9
The Relentless March of Time

Fill in the diagram with the appropriate terms on the right.

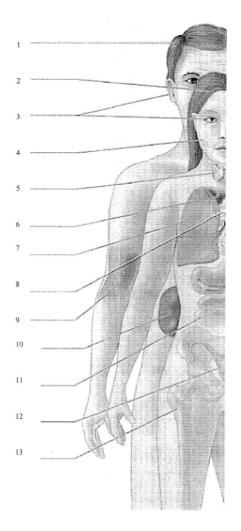

Heart and blood vessels

Kidney and urinary tract

Bones and joints

Skin

Reproductive system

Glands and hormones

Lungs

Hair and nail

Muscles

Brain

Digestive system

Immune system

The senses

Notes:

_____

_____

_____

_____

_____

_____

_____

PowerVisual 10
Processing of Visual Stimuli
Fill in the diagram with the appropriate terms on the right.

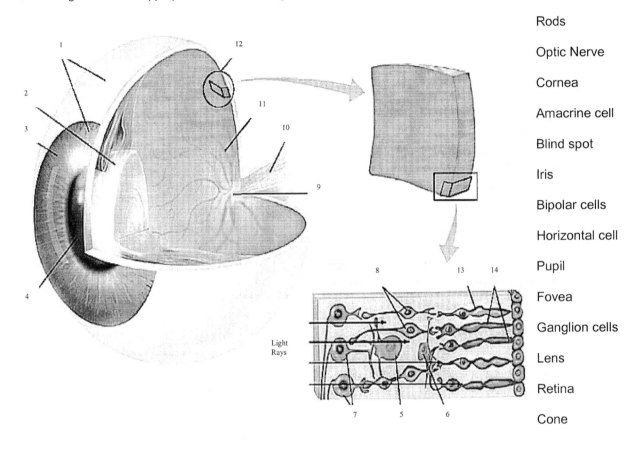

Rods

Optic Nerve

Cornea

Amacrine cell

Blind spot

Iris

Bipolar cells

Horizontal cell

Pupil

Fovea

Ganglion cells

Lens

Retina

Cone

Notes:

_____

_____

_____

_____

_____

_____

_____

_____

PowerVisual 11
The Dark Adaptation Curve
Fill in the diagram with the appropriate terms on the right.

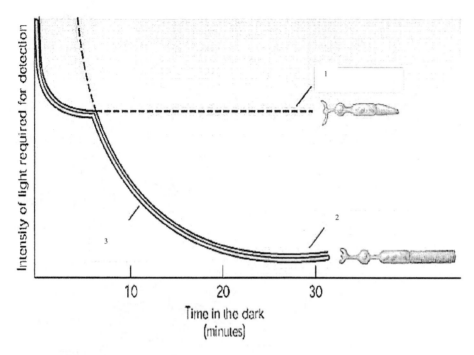

Rod adaptation

Observed adaptation

Cone adaptation

Notes:

_____

_____

_____

_____

_____

_____

_____

_____

_____

_____

_____

_____

PowerVisual 12
Process of Auditory Stimuli
Fill in the diagram with the appropriate terms on the right.

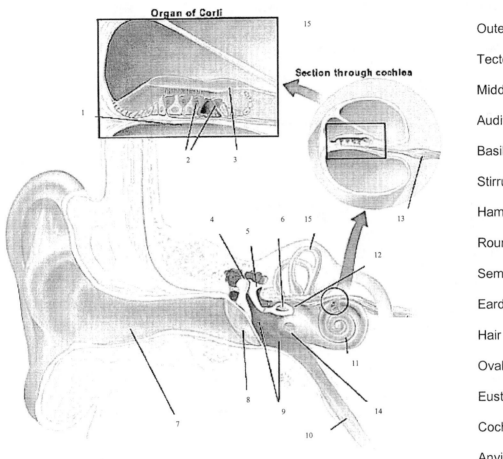

Organ of Corli

Section through cochlea

Outer ear (auditory canal)

Tectorial membrane

Middle ear

Auditory nerve

Basilar membrane

Stirrup (stapes)

Hammer (malleus)

Round window

Semicircular canals

Eardurm

Hair cells

Oval window

Eustachian tube

Cochlea

Anvil (incus)

Notes:

_____

_____

_____

_____

_____

_____

PowerVisual 13
The Stages of Sleep
Fill in the diagram with the appropriate terms on the right.

1 _____
(low amplitude, high frequency)

Awake

7 _____
(higher amplitude, slower frequency)

NREM
Sleep

2 _____
(low frequency, low amplitude)

Sleep spindle   K complex

5 _____
and the K complex

3 _____ (low frequency,
high amplitude)

4 _____
continue to increase
in amplitude

REM Sleep

(occurs when we re-enter
Stage 1, about 90 minutes
after falling asleep
— frequently called
"paradoxical sleep")

6 _____
patterns are very similar
to those of initial
NREM Stage 1

Stage 1 sleep-theta waves

Stage 4-delta waves

Awake-beta waves

REM sleep-brain wave

Stage 3 sleep-beginning of
delta waves

Stage 2 sleep-sleep spindles

Drowsy-alpha waves

Notes:

_____

_____

_____

_____

_____

_____

_____

_____

_____

PowerVisual 14

Pavlov's Classical Conditioning Experiment
Fill in the diagram with the appropriate terms on the right.

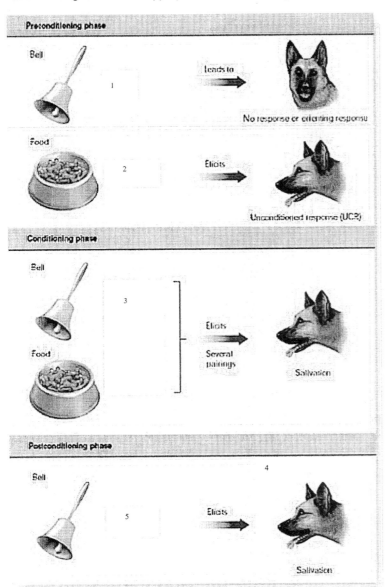

Conditioned stimulus (CS)

Neutral stimulus

Neutral stimulus
+
Unconditioned stimulus

Unconditioned stimulus

Conditioned response (CR)

Notes:

_____

_____

_____

_____

PowerVisual 15
Positive versus Negative Reinforcers
Fill in the diagram with the appropriate terms on the right.

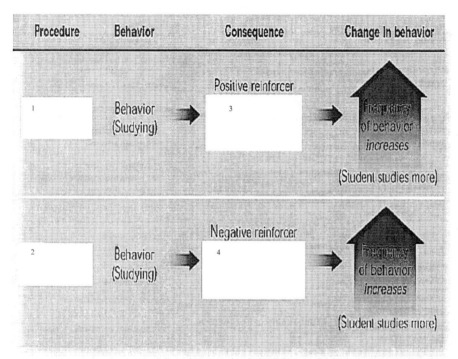

Procedure	Behavior	Consequence	Change in behavior

1.

Behavior (Studying)

Positive reinforcer

3.

Frequency of behavior *increases*

(Student studies more)

2.

Behavior (Studying)

Negative reinforcer

4.

Frequency of behavior *increases*

(Student studies more)

Use of positive reinforcement

Use of negative reinforcement

(Teacher approval) is presented when student studies

(Teacher disapproval) is removed when student studies

Notes:

_____

_____

_____

_____

_____

_____

_____

_____

_____

_____

PowerVisual 16
Negative Reinforcers versus Punishments.
Fill in the diagram with the appropriate terms on the right.

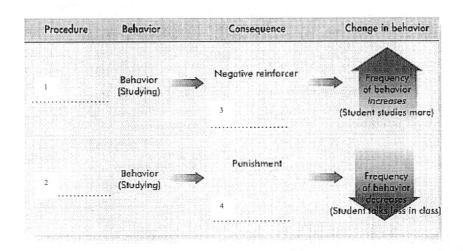

Procedure	Behavior	Consequence	Change in behavior
1	Behavior (Studying)	Negative reinforcer 3	Frequency of behavior increases (Student studies more)
2	Behavior (Studying)	Punishment 4	Frequency of behavior decreases (Student talks less in class)

(Teacher approval)
is presented when student
studies

Use of punishment

(Teacher disapproval)
is removed when student
studies

Use of negative reinforcement

Notes:

_____

_____

_____

_____

_____

_____

_____

_____

_____

PowerVisual 17
Negative Reinforcers versus Punishments.
Fill in the diagram with the appropriate terms on the right.

Episodic memories

Retrospective memories

Semantic memories

Prospective memories

Explicit memories

Implicit memories

Notes:

_____

_____

_____

_____

_____

_____

_____

_____

PowerVisual 18
Maslow's Hierarchy of Needs
Fill in the diagram with the appropriate terms on the right.

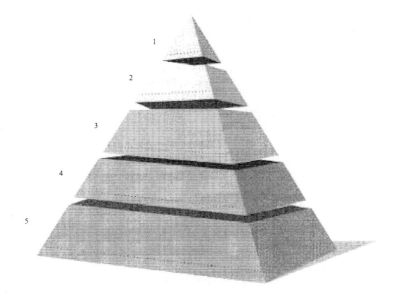

Love and belongingness

Safety needs

Self-actualization

Physiological needs

Esteem needs

Notes:

_____

_____

_____

_____

_____

_____

_____

_____

PowerVisual 19
James-Lange Theory of Emotion
Fill in the diagram with the appropriate terms on the right.

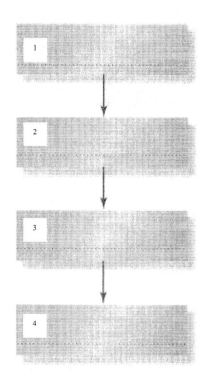

Experiencing the specific emotion

External stimulus

Appraisal of arousal and action

Arousal and action

Notes:

_____

_____

_____

_____

_____

_____

_____

_____

PowerVisual 20
Cannon-Bard Theory of Emotion
Fill in the diagram with the appropriate terms on the right.

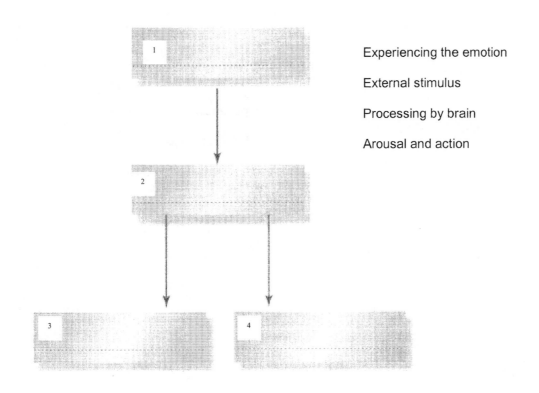

Experiencing the emotion

External stimulus

Processing by brain

Arousal and action

Notes:

_____

_____

_____

_____

_____

_____

_____

_____

PowerVisual 21
Cognitive Appraisal Theory of Emotion
Fill in the diagram with the appropriate terms on the right.

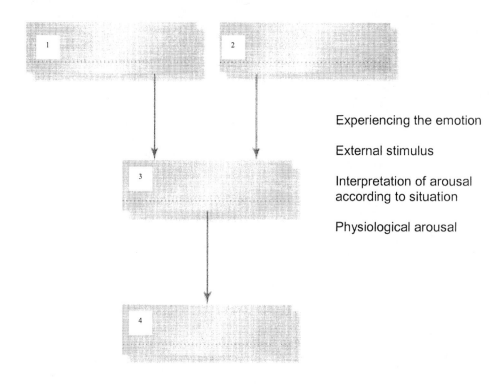

Experiencing the emotion

External stimulus

Interpretation of arousal according to situation

Physiological arousal

Notes:

_____

_____

_____

_____

_____

_____

_____

_____

Answer Key

PowerVisual 1
1) Psychological theory, daily experiences, commonly held beliefs
2) Research questions
3) Hypothesis
4) Examining the research questions
5) Hypothesis testing
6) Evidence (observation)
7) Drawing conclusions
8) Theory construction or modification
9) New research questions and hypothesesis

PowerVisual 3
1) Peripheral nervous system
2) Central nervous system
3) Somatic system
4) Autonomic system
5) Brain
6) Spinal cord
7) Sympathetic system
8) Parasympathetic system

PowerVisual 5
1) Fish Olfactory lobe
2) Fish cerebrum
3) Fish cortex
4) Reptile Neocortex
5) Reptile Cerebellum
6) Human Cerebrum
7) Reptile Cerebrum
8) Reptile Olfactory lobe
9) Human Cerebellum
10) Human Neocortex
11) Fish Cerebellum

PowerVisual 7
1) Cyngulate Gyrus
2) Fornix
3) Hypothalamus
4) Amygdala
5) Mammilary body
6) Thalamus
7) Hippocampus

PowerVisual 2
1) Axon
2) Axon terminals
3) Dendrites
4) Cell body (soma)
5) Nucleus
6) Myelin sheath
7) Synaptic cleft
8) Receptor sites
9) Neurotransmitters
10) Neural Impulse

PowerVisual 4
1) Constricts pupil
2) Stimulates salivation
3) Constricts bronchi
4) Heartbeat (slows)
5) Stimulates gall bladder
6) Stimulates digestive system
7) Contracts bladder
8) Stimulates erection in males and lubrication in females
9) Dilates pupil
10) Inhibits salivation
11) Relaxes bronchi
12) Heartbeat (accelerates)
13) Glucose released
14) Inhibits digestive activity
15) Relaxes bladder
16) Stimulates ejaculation in the male

PowerVisual 6
1) Corpus callosum
2) Hypothalamus
3) Pituitary gland
4) Cerebrum
5) Thalamus
6) Cerebellum
7) Reticular activating system
8) Pons
9) Medulla

PowerVisual 8
1) Hypothalamus
2) Pituitary
3) Thyroid
4) Adrenals
5) Pancreas
6) Kidneys
7) Ovaries
8) Uterus
9) Testes

PowerVisual 9
1) Hair and Nails
2) Brain
3) The senses
4) Skin
5) Glands and hormones
6) Immune system
7) Lungs
8) Heart and blood vessels
9) Muscles
10) Kidney and urinary tract
11) Digestive system
12) Reproductive system
13) Bones and joints

PowerVisual 10
1) Cornea
2) Lens
3) Iris
4) Pupil
5) Amacrine cell
6) Horizontal cell
7) Ganglion cells
8) Bipolar cells
9) Blind spot
10) Optic nerve
11) Fovea
12) Retina
13) Cone
14) Rods

PowerVisual 11
1) Cone adaptation
2) Rod adaptation
3) Observed adaptation

PowerVisual 12
1) Basilar Membrane
2) Hair cells
3) Tectorial membrane
4) Hammer (malleus)
5) Anvil (incus)
6) Stirrup (stapes)
7) Outer ear (auditory canal)
8) Eardrum
9) Middle ear
10) Eustachian tube
11) Cochlea
12) Oval window
13) Auditory nerve
14) Round window
15) Semicircular canals

PowerVisual 13
1) Awake-beta waves
2) Stage 1 sleep-theta waves
3) Stage 3 sleep- beginning of delta waves
4) REM sleep-brain wave
5) Stage 4 delta waves
6) Stage 2 sleep-sleep spindles
7) Drowsy-alpha waves

PowerVisual 14
1) Neutral stimulus
2) Unconditioned stimulus
3) Neutral stimulus+Unconditioned stimulus
4) Conditioned response (CR)
5) Conditioned stimulus (CS)

PowerVisual 15
1) Use of positive reinforcement
2) Use of negative reinforcemnent
3) (Teacher approval)
4) (Teacher disapproval)

PowerVisual 16
1) Use of negative reinforcement
2) Use of punishment
3) (Teacher disapproval)
4) (Teacher approval)

PowerVisual 17
1) Prospective memories
2) Retrospective memories
3) Explicit memories
4) Implicit memories
5) Episodic memories
6) Semantic memories

PowerVisual 18
1) Self-acutalization
2) Esteem needs
3) Love and belongingness
4) Safety needs
5) Physiological needs

PowerVisual 19
1) External stimulus
2) Arousal and action
3) Appraisal of arousal and action
4) Experiencing the specific emotion

PowerVisual 20
1) External stimulus
2) Processing by brain
3) Arousal and action
4) Experiencing the emotion

PowerVisual 21
1) External stimulus
2) Physiological arousal
3) Interpretation of arousal according to situation
4) Experiencing the emotion